JEEP CJ-5

Limited Edition

1960-1975

Compiled by R M Clarke

ISBN 1 85520 7192

BROOKLANDS BOOKS LTD.
P.O. BOX 146, COBHAM,
SURREY, KT11 1LG. UK
sales@brooklands-books.com

www.brooklands-books.com

A-JPCJ5X1

Printed in China

ACKNOWLEDGEMENTS

Brooklands Books has been publishing compilation road test books on a wide range of makes and models for 50 years and today is the world's largest publisher of such material. For this our thanks go to the group of international authors, photographers and publishers who have supported our reference series by allowing us to include their road tests and other stories. In this case *Car and Driver, Car South Africa, Custom Car, Four Wheel Drive Book, Four Wheeler, 4WD, Hot Rod, Motor, Motor Life, Motor Trend, Off Road Australia, Off-Road Fun Cars, Off-Road Vehicles, PV4* and the *World Car Catalogue.*

R M Clarke

Jeep is one of the most recognised brands in the business, not just the automobile business but all business internationally. It's up there with Coca-Cola, IBM, Ferrari and BMW. Not bad for a brand that evolved out of a war-time demand by the US military for a compact go-anywhere multi-purpose kind of vehicle that quickly became a favourite of the American GIs as well as Allied troops.

Such was the fascination with the wartime workhorse that Willys Motors of Toledo, Ohio decided to continue production with a "civilian" version that became a sales success. The styling, such as it was, remained virtually unchanged as did the four-cylinder side-valve engine and the three-speed manual gearbox with attached transfer case and the semi-elliptic leaf spring suspension front and rear.

Most early sales were to the agricultural and exploration industries who quickly came to appreciate the Jeep's ability to go anywhere with complete reliability even if comfort levels were rudimentary and operating the four-wheel drive system was somewhat crude. The world soon began to appreciate its cheeky character and its indominatable spirit.

However, as the 50s came and went the engine was modernised to feature an F-head (overhead inlet valves, side exhausts) for greater efficiency and there were mild styling changes. By the end of the decade the CJ-5 appeared to replace the Jeep "Universal" that had basically been in production since the end of the war. As an advertising man once said, "When you're on a good thing, stick to it." And Jeep was a master of that.

Despite ever stronger competition from other manufacturers Jeep continued to be the standard-setter in so many ways to those who understood and appreciated what it represented and the fascinating history behind it.

Gavin Farmer

CONTENTS

JEEPING COMES ON *FAST!*

A new car sport in which the machine doesn't have to be a true jeep — just be able to take rough punishment. It's an off-the beaten path challenge of mechanics, driving skill and plain guts

By Robert Ames

LAST February an old prospector and his burro were trudging slowly toward an isolated area in the Southern California high desert. The canyon narrowed and sheer walls jutted up a hundred feet on either side. The last few miles had been particularly rough since huge boulders blocked the way and sharper rocks slipped underfoot.

"It'll be worth it though, Beulah," the prospector said, talking to the burro. "Ain't ever nobody gets back into these here hills. Prospecting should be real good."

He heard a sound.

"That's funny, Beulah. You sounded just like an autymobile horn."

Then the prospector heard a low rumbling and turned around accusing Beulah, but the animal gazed back innocently. The sound continued and grew louder.

"If I didn't know where we was, Beulah, I'd swear that sounded like cars." He paused, thoughtfully. "But that ain't possible!"

He didn't want to believe it either, when a white jeep squeezed by a giant boulder a hundred yards down the wash and headed toward him. But another followed and then another. By the time the first car crawled over the rocks alongside the prospector a dozen jeeps lined the trail.

The lead car was driven by a bronzed man stripped to the waist and wearing a red handkerchief Apache style around his forehead. He stood up, waved to the prospector and shouted:

"Hey, mister, is this the right road to Fargo Canyon?"

The old prospector was still a little shaken when he told me the story a few days later. It was his first experience

WHEN THINGS GET ROUGH EVERYONE, WELL ALMOST EVERYONE, PUSHES. HERE A STATION WAGON IS NEGOTIATED AROUND A SHORT TURN.

JEEPING COMES ON *FAST!*

with jeepers, who are popping up in the damndest places these days. Jeepers are a special breed of motoring enthusiasts and their goal that day was to blaze a trail over a route where no car had ever been driven.

They call their sport "jeeping" and it is probably the most rugged automotive activity found anywhere. No other driving challenge provides a better test of a man and his machine against nature. Jeepers have taken their cars up 90-degree hills (by using a winch), across sandy wastelands, through rivers, down mountain washes, along beaches where they had to duck waves to drive, and through passes hardly an inch wider than their cars. There are few, if any, back trails that a jeeper will not tackle. The worse the road, the happier he feels.

Jeeping got started in World War II when the four-wheel-drive cars proved themselves in the mire of Europe, the deserts of Africa and the jungles of the Pacific. After the war, military jeeps became available on the surplus market. Veterans, who once vowed they would have nothing more to do with jeeps, were among the first to buy the war-weary vehicles. Initially, the plan was to use the car around a ranch or farm and occasionally to get to a remote hunting or fishing area.

But many jeep owners remembered how much the car would do and they began trying other trips. There were hills to climb, streams to ford and back trails to explore.

During the next 10 years thousands of individuals discovered jeeping and eventually small groups began meeting informally for jeeping trips. Around 1950, clubs began to band together officially. About three years ago, jeep clubs started booming and dozens of clubs are formed every year.

The best way to get started in jeeping is to buy a four-wheel-drive car. Perhaps a better word to describe the sport would be "four-wheel driving" and jeepers use the word jeep to refer to any vehicle that has power transmitted to all four wheels. Originally, the word meant only the short wheelbase, open-air military model. Today, when a jeeper wants to specifically refer to the open-air model, he calls it a bobtail jeep.

JEEP CLUB on a high desert road. Stops are frequent to enjoy scenery, climb hills or look for a worse road. Nearly every jeep in this caravan has been modified in one way or another.

Military models are still the jeeper's favorite but the Willys CJ5 is a close second and is becoming more numerous every year. Limited numbers of foreign jeeps are appearing with the Toyopet, Land Rover and DKW heading the list. Willys station wagons are the most common closed-body vehicles with station wagons built on a panel truck body next. Four-wheel-drive pick-ups are seldom seen, but the Willys is the most popular.

Military models probably outnumber all other types of vehicles put together. These are also favorite hop-up cars and under the hood of many are high-powered V-8 engines. Even CJ5's, which have the F-head four-cylinder engine, have usually been subjected to a lot of the hot rodder's techniques.

Jeepers have learned many things about hopping up their engines and have found that what is good engineering practice for sports cars, hot rods or racing cars is not necessarily the best procedure for jeeps. One vital difference was discovered the hard way by a North Hollywood, California, jeeper who installed a powerful Corvette V-8 engine with a racing cam and performance modifications. He had plenty of power but the engine idled too fast for a slow start—one of the first lessons of back country driving. When he engaged the clutch, his drive shaft snapped. Result, the racing cam came out and the engine was slightly detuned. Then the jeeper got what he wanted, power in the low-range rpm, plus faster speed on the highway.

Performance, while not the most important factor in jeeping, is not entirely overlooked by the modification enthusiast. A change in the entire power train sometimes has more to do with performance than merely installing a larger engine. One jeep recently clocked over 100 mph for a standing quarter-mile at a drag strip; the following week the same jeep was negotiating a back-country wash. This jeeper equipped his car with a Studebaker overdrive transmission plus a V-8 engine.

Another jeeper showed up on a cross-country with a modified station wagon. Inside was an airplane instrument panel, with a two-way radio, compass, altimeter and several other instruments. Under the hood was a Buick V-8 engine and coupled to the powerplant was a dynaflow transmission which operated in four-wheel drive.

Modifications are not limited to the power train and the lists of the changes that jeepers make include installing a Hudson steering column, complete changes in the suspension, roll bars, channel iron bars running from the front to rear fenders (to hold the jeep together while jumping), bigger tires and dozens of other changes all designed to make the jeep more versatile and rugged.

After getting into a four-wheel-drive car, a new jeeper soon tires of the ordinary back-country road. Before long, he calls any trail that can be negotiated with a two-wheel drive pickup a freeway. The jeeper has a car that will go anywhere and wants to prove it. What he wants is a really rugged road, or better yet, no road at all.

The best and quickest way to find America's worst roads is to join a jeep club. The most important club function is to provide and to organize jeep trips. A jeep trip is usually "discovered" in one of two ways. A member goes along with another jeep club or a few members scout an entirely new route in their own jeeps. After a trip has been selected, the caravan is organized much along the order of the old-time covered wagon trains across the West.

The member who originally scouted the trip becomes wagon

MAN AND MAN'S best friend tackle jeeping's most difficult task, cross-country in the sand. A few minutes later they were stuck and waiting for a jeeper's best friend—the winch.

JEEP CLUBS are frequently called on for emergency jobs a regular car could not possibly do. California club members formed a ground rescue squad and work with CAP and sheriff's office.

master and leads the way. Each jeep packs its own camping gear and food supplies. Bringing up the rear is a jeep in good repair, usually with a supply of tools and a few spare parts. It is his job to see that no one gets left behind.

Jeep trips have one thing in common—they are all made over the most primitive road conditions possible. A popular Western trip is down a wash or canyon. If a jeep club can find a wash near the top of a mountain that is at least as wide as a jeep, it is in business. From there the trip starts. Waterfalls, or more accurately the rocks over which water falls when there is any, are the chief challenge on a wash trip. Unfortunately, or fortunately, as the jeeper sees it, water usually picks a waterfall to make a sharp bend.

Bobtails rarely have trouble, but station wagons seldom turn quickly enough for a waterfall bend. The usual procedure is for everyone to get on one side and push the rear end over to help the wagon negotiate the turn.

Rocks are a constant menace and it takes skillful driving to hit them at just the right place. If, for example, a rock would drag on the axle, or bell housing, the procedure is to go over another rock with one wheel throwing the part in danger higher.

Sandy deserts are found in the west from Nebraska to California and from Texas to the Canadian border. These are other playgrounds for the jeeper. Sand calls for different tactics and different tires. In recent years, smoother and bigger tires have become standard items.

Another frequent jeep trip is in the bed of a river, exploring it as far as possible. In hot weather, the forests and high mountains are popular. During winter, roads that never see a snow plow are the most often driven.

The organization and discipline that jeepers learn on their trips pays off in another way. In times of emergency and disaster, they work as volunteer groups, driving their jeeps to areas inaccessible to standard cars.

The Hillhoppers of Oakland, California, are members of a civil defense unit and have trained through the Red Cross to be better qualified in an emergency. Furthermore, they are

course, mud racing, slalom-in-the-sea and hill climbing.

While some localities like Truth or Consequences, New Mexico, have regularly scheduled racing, competition is only occasionally offered as public exhibitions. For the most part "roadeos" are an impromptu occasion staged in an outdoor location near where a jeep club is camping for the night. The type of event depends on finding a favorable location.

The broad jump is a good example of these informal contests. This takes a low, fairly firm piece of ground that rises gently, then drops sharply three or four feet. Jeepers back off, take a run and let their jeeps sail through the air. Hill climbing is usually a part of every caravan and hardly any jeeper can pass up an opportunity to try a hill that angles up more than 45 degrees.

Obstacle courses and mud races are found most often in regularly scheduled roadeos and are similar to England's field trials—with a few variations that are strictly American. The Yakima Ridgerunners have produced three public roadeos and their course is typical. A quarter-mile track is soaked with water for several days leaving deep water hazards with plenty of mud, then obstacles are placed on the track, including several broad jumps over the water.

Competition is not universally practiced by all jeepers and many prefer the challenge of the back road rather than pitting jeep against jeep. The answer seems to be that some of the sports are just too rough on the cars. Jumping, for instance, can leave the front axle looking more like a valentine than something an automobile manufacturer would recognize. But jeepers have a strange way of compromising themselves in this case. A jeeper who swears he will not jump in competition will never hesitate an instant if jumping is necessary to negotiate a bad road.

There seems to be nothing that a jeeper will not try and he will travel nearly any distance to try it. A Washington club goes regularly to New Mexico, Californians make treks to the Canadian border and a Colorado cavalcade attracts many middle-western and eastern jeepers. One club in central California even

They're after the roughest trail, the hardest ride

active in a tree planting program helping to reforest burned-out areas.

The Ridgerunners in San Diego County, California, also assist the Red Cross. In one emergency trip, they carried food and fuel to elderly women snowbound in the mountains. Cooperating with the sheriff's department, they have driven their jeeps on several missions searching for lost persons. In 1958 they were asked by the Civil Air Patrol to help in rescue work. They formed a ground rescue squadron of 16 jeeps equipped with two-way radios and first-aid equipment.

Another jeep club with the same name, Ridgerunners, but based in Yakima, Washington, have had their share of emergency service. Their list of accomplishments includes bringing men and equipment into remote areas to fight forest fires, locating crashed airplanes, finding lost hunters and rescue work during floods.

While emergency service is more exciting and appeals to a true jeeper, public service is also another important activity for jeep clubs. The Tulare County California Four-Wheel-Drive Club, for instance, has equipped several jeeps with two-way radios and serve not only in times of emergency but during celebrations, parades and other events.

Besides public service and rugged outdoor trips, jeepers have still another exciting outlet for their energies—competitive sports. These occasions are probably America's most spectacular automotive events and include such tests as broad jumping, obstacle

has plans for a four-month jeep caravan to South America.

Why this tremendous upsurge of interest in jeeping? If you want to be analytical, there are literally dozens of reasons. It could be compared to a poker game where the limit has been taken off. There is practically no limit to where a car with four-wheel-drive can go. (And I know hundreds of jeepers who are trying to take "practically" out of that sentence.) There are no displacement or horsepower ratings to worry about. Four-cylinder bobtails frequently challenge V-8's to cross-country duels—and win as often as not. And there is no limit as to who can play the game. The whole family can enjoy jeeping at the same time.

But I know the real reason—and so does any jeeper. Ask any enthusiast and he will tell you exactly why he does it: "Jeeping is a hell of a lot of fun." •

DRIVING WILLYS' CJ-5 UNIVERSAL JEEP

by Bob Ames

FOR THE PAST MONTH I have driven a Willys CJ-5 Jeep Universal. This car was not a run-of-the-production-line car — but was, in my opinion, the best all-around Jeep for the average back-country driver.

There were three major optional items, and each will be discussed later with the reasons why I think it improves the stock Jeep. These options were: in front, a Koenig winch; in the center, a four-speed transmission; and in the rear, a 4.27-to-1 axle ratio.

For those who are not familiar with the mechanical components, here is a brief rundown: The Jeep is powered by an F-head, four-cylinder engine displacing 134 cubic inches and producing 72 hp at 4,000 rpm. The carburetor is a single-barrel, and the compression ratio is 6.9-to-1, which gives the car excellent tolerance to low-octane fuels.

Like any conventional car with manual shift, power is directed through the transmission, but here the similarity ends. From the transmission it is taken through a transfer case, where it may be transmitted directly to the rear wheels or multiplied again and divided equally between the rear and front wheels. Or, the transfer case can be put in neutral, and another lever engaged and the engine power directed to the winch. In other words, there are three choices of using the power: conventional drive, four-wheel drive or operating the winch. To control the power output there are four levers: a conventional manual shift, a front axle shift, an underdrive and a PTO shift.

The ride is best described as a "rump" ride. It is harsh over almost any type of terrain, but the new seats in the CJ-5 are a great improvement in smoothing out the worst of the ride. From the standpoint of purpose, this ride is entirely justifiable. There are seven leaf springs in front and nine in the rear. This gives the CJ-5 a payload of 1500 pounds — better than most conventional station wagons. Naturally, it is bound to ride stiff. On the other hand, I drove this Jeep over a rocky, washboard road at 30 mph — a trip which would have shaken many conventional cars to little pieces in less than a mile.

Acceleration of this CJ-5 was down from its normal potential. This is only a natural result of the 4.27 axle ratio. I would judge acceleration to be equal to the slower compacts.

Gas mileage is the hardest figure to report. I recorded a range from 10 to 20 mpg. The 10-mpg figure included mostly compound-low, four-wheel driving with some winching. The 20-mpg figure was nearly all highway driving. Overall average for 1500 miles, which included all types of gearing and some winching, was 15.5 mpg. This is exceptionally good, considering the types of terrain driven during the test.

Those who are accustomed to Detroit's plushier products might be a little shocked at the Jeep's interior. Perhaps the most revealing thing is that so much of the interior is also the exterior. Not only is instrumentation at a bare minimum, there are virtually no decorations at all. Everything about the Jeep is picked not for decor, but for durability.

The Jeep is probably the only Detroit car that is designed without a top and without doors. But there are about a dozen tops available optionally — from all-metal jobs to the new convertible canvas outfit which was on the test Jeep. It has a wide, zippered rear door which can be rolled up for full-open back space. The doors are removable to give about 50 per cent open space. Or in about five minutes one man can take the top down (or put it up) and fold the windshield down for completely open-air traveling.

As mentioned earlier, this Jeep had three options which I believe improve its

New convertible top in last stage of going down. Top folds down and entire unit folds. Doors are detachable.

practicality a good deal. The standard rear axle ratio, 5.38, was changed to 4.27-to-1. And the three-speed transmission, with ratios of 2.798, 1.551 and 1, was eliminated in favor of the four-speed option with ratios of 6.398, 3.092, 1.686 and 1. Reverse jumped from 3.798 to 7.820. To show how this improves the two most important driving characteristics of a Jeep, low-speed power and top speed, it is necessary to resort to mathematical formulas.

Maximum top speed with the 4.27 is 77 mph; with the 5.38 it drops to 65 mph. Allowing for the effect of variables, or about 85 per cent efficiency, this means that a practical top speed would be 65 mph with the optional axle, opposed to 52 mph with the standard. The only disadvantage to the 4.27 is slowing down for long hills. But during the test, hills didn't make any significant difference in the time it took to make a long trip, although the top speed did.

To show just how much low-gear performance is improved with the four-speed transmission, it is necessary to compute the grade ability in per cent, which is the grade on which the Jeep will start or the grade it will climb after it is started. First of all, look at the change in overall ratio in compound low: 68-to-1 for the four-speed and 4.27 axle, compared to 38-to-1 for the standard axle and three-speed transmission.

In computing the grade ability I have used maximum torque, 114 lbs.-ft., 85 per cent efficiency, total ratio, a road resistance factor for good gravel surface, 14-inch loaded radius for the tires (6.70 x 15, another option) and a payload of approximately 750 pounds.

Mathematically, the grade that the test Jeep would climb would be a 168-percent or about 59-degree hill. A stock Jeep under similar circumstances has a maximum potential of 94 per cent or about 43 degrees. This is the best way the difference in power potential between the two models can be stated.

This may explain why I prefer the 4.27 axle with a four-speed transmission. Top speed is about 15 mph better, while the low-gear performance is almost doubled. And although these mathematical figures are theoretical, the test proved them to be just as practical on the road.

Just a word of caution though. The trucker or experienced Jeeper will have no difficulty in using these figures. They will treat them as comparative ratios between the two cars, which the figures are. The fellow who tries to climb a 59-degree hill will undoubtedly get more than he bargained for. There are simply too many variables: the road surface may be poorer, the front wheels may lift, the carburetor may flood, the fuel pump may quit, the payload may be heavier. Granted the potential is there, but for practical purposes it boils down to the fact that the four-speed transmission increases the power.

The third major option on the test car was the Koenig winch. I am going to discuss it only as extra weight in this article. In a later issue I intend to get deep into the subject of winching with this winch, and the areas to be covered (deadman, anchor stakes, snatch blocks, A-frame, doubling winch power, etc.) will fill another column. But the change that the winch makes in performance alone is worthy of mention.

Logically, any four-wheel-drive car works better when the weight is distributed equally over the four wheels. Unloaded, a Jeep has about 58 per cent of its weight on the front wheels, but since the payload puts most of its weight on the rear wheels, this ratio changes rapidly. When climbing a hill the front wheels have a tendency to lift. The extra weight of a winch helps keep them down — one of the most important factors in climbing hills. Loaded, the test Jeep had no difficulty with some very steep hills encountered during back-country driving. /MT

Iron rods support front section of top. Here doors are off and back is rolled up for medium open-air use.

The Jeep at its best. From full top, big photo on opposite page, to bobtail style takes about five minutes.

A new overhead cam six-cylinder engine that promises much for back country enthusiasts

WILLYS NEW 140hp BOMB

One of the biggest news items for four-wheel drive enthusiasts this year was the announcement in May that Willys Motors would offer a new, more powerful Six. But most important, the new engine has an overhead cam that is exclusive in its field and gives the Willy's powerplant dozens of advantages that are going to pay off in back country driving.

The new engine is officially called the "Tornado-OHC" by Willys. It is being offered initially in only five models of the line. These are the four-wheel drive Jeep utility wagon, one-ton pickup truck and panel delivery, the two-wheel drive Jeep station wagon and sedan delivery. Of these outfits, the most popular among four wheelers is the 4wd wagon.

For those who are interested in figures, the Toledo engineers rate the Tornado OHC at 140 hp at 4000 rpm with torque of 210 lbs. ft. peaking at 1750 rpm. This means the new ohc Six is going to be working at top efficiency in the low rpm ranges — where it counts in a back country situation.

The overhead cam design eliminates many valve train components — including push rods, lifters, followers, etc., that are found in most overhead valve engines. This coupled with the fact that lightweight die-cast aluminum components are used extensively, brings up another feature that will be of more than passing interest to the conversion enthusiast. The new engine weighs in at less than 550 pounds, substantially under other engines of comparable power — and considerably under V-8's.

Among the many components made of aluminum are the oil and water pumps, camshaft bearing support deck, rocker arm cover, intake manifold and front accessory cover. The block is cast iron.

But there are many other advantages to the new Willys engine that might be overlooked by the fellow who has only a casual acquaintance with tuning-up and repairing his own engine. The overhead camshaft is directly responsible for most of these.

All components of the valve train system — valves, valve parts, camshaft, bearing support deck and rocker arms — are

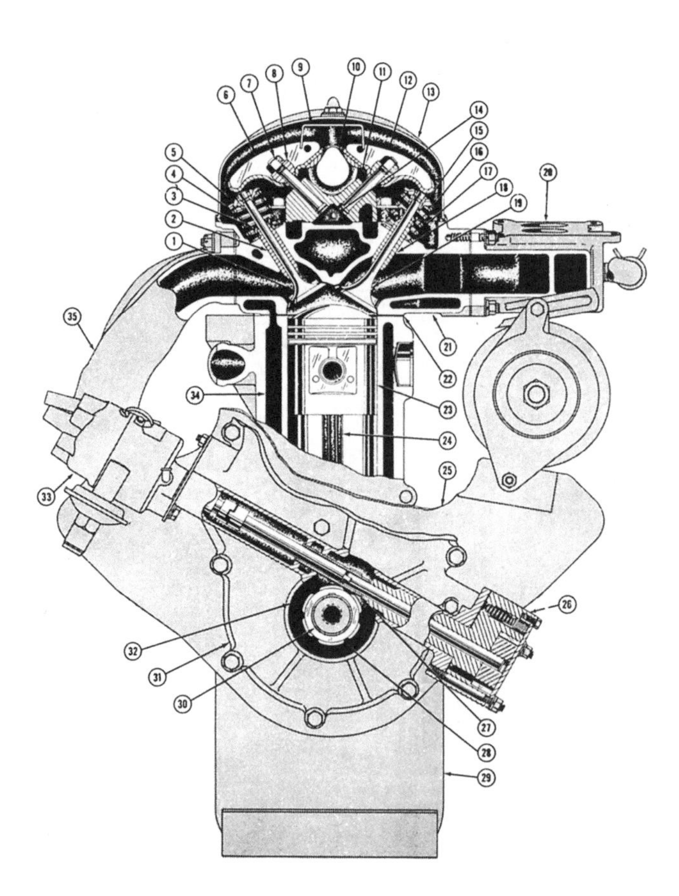

Front Sectional View
1—Exhaust Valve
2—Exhaust Valve Guide
3—Valve Guide Seal
4—Valve Spring
5—Exhaust Valve Spring Guide
6—Rocker Arm
7—Rocker Arm Stud
8—Rocker Arm Ball
9—Rocker Arm Guide
10—Camshaft
11—Cam Bearing Support Deck
12—Intake Rocker Arm
13—Rocker Arm Cover
14—Lubrication Pipe
15—Valve Spring Guide
16—Valve Spring
17—Valve Guide Seal
18—Intake Valve Guide
19—Intake Valve
20—Intake Manifold
21—Cylinder Head
22—Cylinder Head Gasket
23—Piston
24—Connecting Rod
25—Front Engine Plate
26—Oil Pump
27—Oil Pump Helical Gear
28—Oil Pump Drive Gear
29—Oil Pan
30—Crankshaft
31—Timing Chain Cover
32—Timing Chain Cover Oil Seal
33—Distributor
34—Cylinder Block
35—Exhaust Manifold

Side Sectional View
1—Cooling Fan
2—Fan Drive Pulley
3—Water Pump
4—Timing Chain
5—Camshaft Sprocket
6—Fuel Pump Eccentric
7—Camshaft
8—Cam Bearing Support Deck
9—Rocker Arm Cover
10—Intake Manifold
11—Lubrication Tube
12—Cylinder Head
13—Core Plug
14—Cylinder Block
15—Starting Motor
16—Clutch Housing
17—Filler Block Guard
18—Upper Rear Oil Seal
19—Clutch
20—Lower Rear Oil Seal
21—Rear Filler Block
22—Oil Pan Seal
23—Rear Main Bearing
24—Rear Main Bearing Cap
25—Oil Intake Screen
26—Oil Pan
27—Connecting Rod Bearing Cap
28—Oil Intake Pipe
29—Intermediate Main Bearing Cap Screw
30—Intermediate Main Bearing Cap
31—Dip Stick Guide
32—Breather Cap
33—Oil Filter
34—Crankshaft
35—Front Filler Block
36—Oil Pan Seal
37—Front Engine Plate
38—Front Main Bearing Cap
39—Front Main Bearing
40—Timing Chain Sprocket
41—Oil Pump Drive Gear
42—Oil Slinger
43—Timing Chain Cover Oil Seal
44—Vibration Damper
45—Oil Fitting
46—Timing Chain Cover
47—Connecting Rod
48—Piston
49—Piston Pin

mounted on the cylinder head. This means that regular maintenance jobs, like adjusting the valves becomes simplicity itself. Just lift the valve cover, grab a wrench and go to work. And for more involved jobs, like grinding the valves, the entire cylinder head assembly with the cam can be removed as a unit for bench servicing.

The new Six's pistons are dome shaped, and the combustion chamber has a semi-spherical design which produces what engineers call a controlled turbulence, or more simply, a swirl pattern for the fuel as it is compressed. Generally, experts agree that this provides maximum combustion efficiency. It also allows for larger valves and permits maximum cooling around the valves. This means that in a back country situation the throttle can be pushed down and the engine responds better. A big advantage in climbing a hill.

Displacement of the new engine is 230-cubic-inches, with a bore and stroke of 3.34x4.38 inches. The compression ratio is 8.5-to-1 which means the engine will run best on regular fuel.

There was not enough time between the Four Wheeler's deadline and the release date of the new Six to make a detailed technical analysis in depth. But the information here covers most of the major details for enthusiasts. As soon as a four-wheel drive car with the Tornado OHC is available, a complete test will be conducted and the results reported.

From our brief analysis of the specifications, only two disappointments are evident. As yet it is not available in the FC series and not in the CJ-5 Universal.

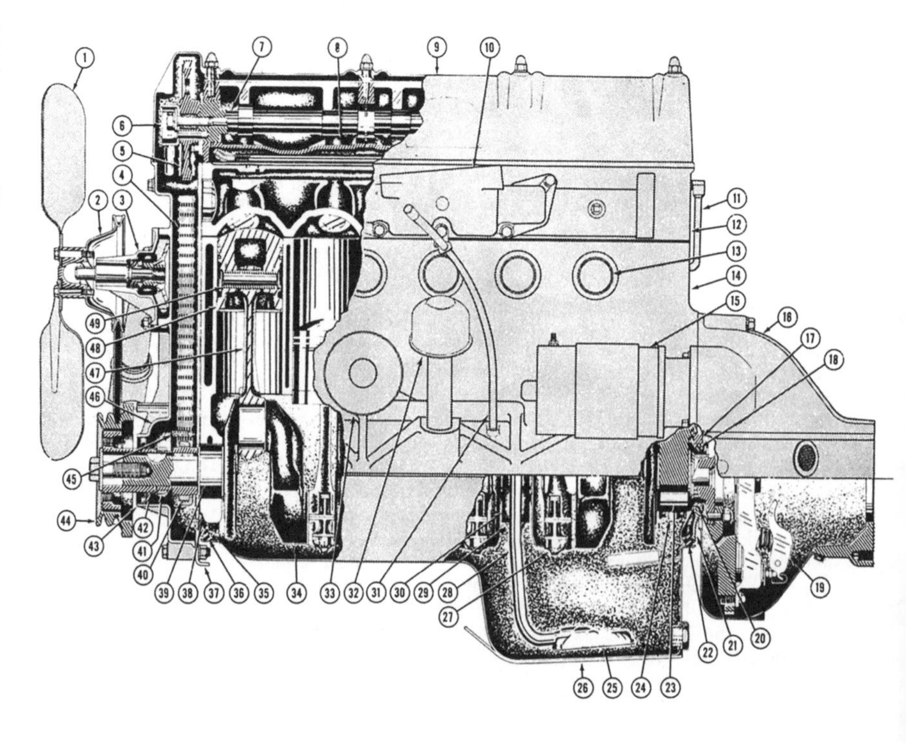

BUICK V-6 CONVERSION IN A CJ-5

When Buick introduced their V-6 last year the engine set off a storm of controversy among conversion enthusiasts. We here at the FOUR WHEELER have listened to these arguments, and have even ventured a few opinions ourselves. There are of some of these conversions around already, but until this month there has not been an opportunity to examine this particular conversion close up and drive the car. As a result, up to now everything has been an educated guess.

However, we recently had a chance to photograph and drive Lou DeWolfe's V-6 conversion near his home in West Covina. The conversion is well done, and Lou has shown a lot of excellent horse sense in mating the new powerplant to his present running gear. And after driving his outfit we are convinced that the V-6 conversion is going to become extremely popular — and may even gain as much favor as the ubiquitous Chevrolet 283 V-8.

Lou started with the Buick V-6 and mated it to his present transmission with a Hoosier conversion kit. The engine has had a little hopping up and now boasts Belinger headers and Mitchell glass packs. The carburetor was changed to a Buick Electra two-barrel with 1-3/16" venturii. The air cleaner is the largest Buick has to offer. These changes have increased the power of the V-6 to 163 hp.

The radiator was swapped for a 'Jeep' tropical radiator which is three inches thick and requires virtually no adapting to set in the CJ-5. The fan was borrowed from a refrigeration unit and with its six blades pumps more than enough air.

Perhaps the most remarkable feature of the conversion is that the Six weighs 78 pounds less than the Four it replaced. This means Lou has more than doubled his power while reducing his weight.

In deciding on his overall ratio, Lou decided to stick with the present 5.38 axle and add a Rancho overdrive with a dash-mounted button. This means he can shift in and out of overdrive at will. The V-6 will tool along at 60 mph and still have plenty left for passing on a long hill.

Among the other goodies he has installed are a Hudson steering column, 11-inch brakes from a 'Jeep' station wagon, Chrysler wheels, warn hubs, easy-eye windshield and a micro-brake lock.

There are two interesting features about the steering. Lou is probably the first four wheeler to discover that the Scout stering wheel fits the Hudson steering column and is far superior to the Hudson steering wheel. But the most important thing about the steering is something that will interest all enthusiasts.

He has adapted a shock absorber to work as front end stabilizer and this has a remarkable effect. Shocks that are ordinarily transmitted through the steering wheel are virtually eliminated, making back country trails far easier and much less fatiguing.

The antenna on the rear of his rig is for his amateur radio outfit. For other four wheelers who might be "hams," Lou has a general license and his call letters are WA6AGW.

BLAZE A TRAIL WITH THE NEW 'Jeep' Camper

FITS ANY V-6 POWERED CJ-5 'JEEP' UNIVERSAL.

Camping enthusiasts, here's the greatest idea in trailblazing rigs since the horse and buggy. Now, you can combine the famous go-anywhere, do-anything 'Jeep' Universal with a brand new, attachable, family-sized, slip-on camper, featuring a 2-tone, all weather exterior, with the very latest in styling. Inside you'll find a completely self-contained camping unit. The type that permits passengers to travel inside. It's spacious, family-sized, with sleeping room for four. There's a beautiful kitchen area complete with running water, built-in cabinets, and an oven, stove, and hood package. You'll also find a marine-type toilet, outside electrical hook-up facilities, and many, many other fine camping features.

THERE'S REALLY NOTHING LIKE THE NEW 'JEEP' CAMPER

With the 'Jeep' Universal and Camper combination, you're not limited to the highways. 'Jeep' 4-wheel drive sees to that. Get off the road, pick out your site, and set up camp. On location, the camper is easily detached from the 'Jeep' Universal. And that means in a few short minutes you've got a vacation home that doesn't have to move until you say the word. Your 'Jeep' Universal is free for more adventure. More hillsides to climb. Or even a short trip back to the country store. But returning to your completely undisturbed campsite is the most rewarding part of all.

Campers, whether you follow the road map or follow your nose, you'll never have a chance for more fun than with the 4-wheel drive 'Jeep' Universal and the all new 'Jeep' Camper. Blaze a trail to your nearby 'Jeep' recreational dealer soon.

YOU'VE GOT TO DRIVE IT TO BELIEVE IT

Take it . . . or leave it! On location, the 'Jeep' Camper unit can easily be detached from the 'Jeep' Universal.

Discover the real campsites with the famous 'Jeep' Universal and the new 'Jeep' Camper.

Kaiser Jeep

CJ-5 JEEP Universal

ENGINE CAPACITY 134.20 cu in, 2,194.17 cu cm
FUEL CONSUMPTION 25.7 m/imp gal, 21.4 m/US gal, 11 l x 100 km
SEATS 5 - 6 **MAX SPEED** 90 mph, 144.9 km/h
PRICE –

ENGINE front, 4 stroke; cylinders: 4, vertical, in line; bore and stroke: 3.25 × 4.37 in, 82.5 × 111 mm; engine capacity: 134.20 cu in, 2,194.17 cu cm; compression ratio: 7.4; max power (SAE): 75 hp at 4,000 rpm; max torque (SAE): 114 lb/ft, 15.7 kg/m at 2,000 rpm; max number of engine rpm: 5,000; specific power: 34.2 hp/l; cylinder block: cast iron; cylinder head: cast iron; crankshaft bearings: 3; valves: 2 per cylinder, overhead, parallel, push-rods and rockers; camshaft: 1, side; lubrication: rotary pump, full flow filter; lubricating system capacity: 8.27 imp pt, 10 US pt, 4.7 l; carburation: 1 downdraught single barrel carburettor; fuel feed: mechanical pump; cooling system: water; cooling system capacity: 14 imp pt, 16.70 US pt, 7.9 l.

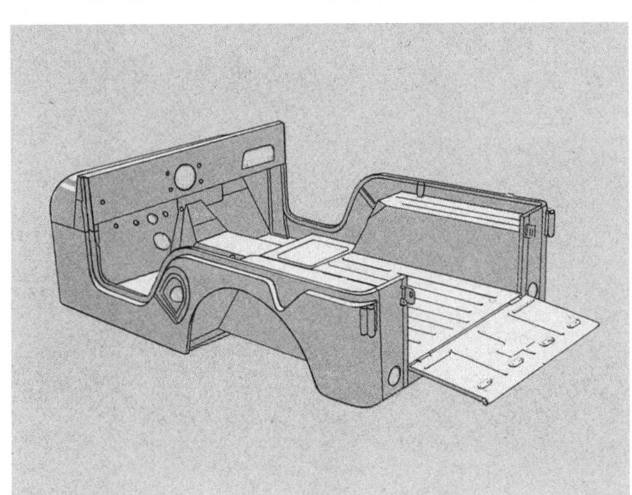

TRANSMISSION driving wheels: front (automatically engaged with transfer box low ratio) and rear; clutch: single dry plate; gearbox: mechanical; gears: 3 with high and low ratios + reverse; synchromesh gears: II, III; gearbox ratios: I 3.339 (low 5.80), II 1.551 (low 4.01), III 1, rev 3.798 (low 6.26); gear lever and low ratio lever: central; final drive: hypoid bevel; axle ratio: 4.27.

CHASSIS box-type ladder frame, lateral members; front suspension: rigid axle, semi-elliptic leafsprings, telescopic dampers; rear suspension: rigid axle, semi-elliptic leafsprings, telescopic dampers.

STEERING cam and peg; turns of steering wheel lock to lock: 2.58.

BRAKES drum, 2 front leading shoes; braking surface: total 102.65 sq in, 662.09 sq cm.

ELECTRICAL EQUIPMENT voltage: 12 V; battery: 50 Ah; headlights: 2.

DIMENSIONS AND WEIGHT wheel base: 81 in, 2,507 mm; front track: 48.44 in, 1,230 mm; rear track: 48.44 in, 1,230 mm; overall length: 135.56 in, 3,443 mm; overall width: 68.88 in, 1,749 mm; overall height: 70 in, 1,778 mm; dry weight: 2,278 lb, 1,033 kg; turning circle (between walls): 35.2 ft, 10.7 m; tyres: 6.00 × 16; fuel tank capacity: 8.8 imp gal, 10.5 US gal, 40 l.

BODY estate car; doors: 4 + 1; seats: 5 - 6; front seats: separate.

PERFORMANCE max speeds: 26 mph, 41.9 km/h in 1st gear; 56 mph, 90.2 km/h in 2nd gear; 90 mph, 144.9 km/h in 3rd gear; power-weight ratio 30.4 lb/hp, 13.8 kg/hp; carrying capacity: 1,058 lb, 480 kg; speed in direct drive at 1,000 rpm: 19.3 mph, 31.1 km/h.

PRACTICAL INSTRUCTIONS fuel: 90 oct petrol; engine sump oil: 6.69 imp pt, 4 US pt, 3.8 l, SAE 20, change every 3,000 miles, 4,800 km; gearbox oil: 1.40 imp pt, 1.70 US pt, 0.8 l, SAE 90, change every 12,000 miles, 19,300 km; final drive oil: 1.40 imp pt, 1.70 US pt, 0.8 l, SAE 90, change every 6,000 miles, 9,700 km; greasing: every 1,000-6,000 miles, 1,600-9,700 km, 33 points; tappet clearances: inlet 0.018 in, 0.46 mm, exhaust 0.016 in, 0.41 mm; valve timing: inlet opens 9° before tdc and closes 50° after bdc, exhaust opens 47° before bdc and closes 12° after tdc; tyre pressure (medium load): front 26 psi, 1.8 atm, rear 24 psi, 1.7 atm.

VARIATIONS AND OPTIONAL ACCESSORIES 7.00 × 16 tyres; 4-speed mechanical gearbox (I 6.398, II 3.092, III 1.686, IV 1, rev 7.820); Perkins Diesel engine, capacity 192.40 cu in, 3,145.74 cu cm, bore and stroke 3.50 × 5 in, 88.9 × 127 mm, max power (SAE) 60 hp at 3,000 rpm, 16.5 compression ratio.

JEEP WITH V-6 MUSCLE

M/T ROAD TEST

REVISITING the Jeep every year or so is a therapy recommended for the most of us who between times aim air-conditioned sedans down the highway.

Not that the Jeep wasn't air-conditioned! It came to us in bare-bones form when winter was still lingering, and the extra-cost top and side curtains were not included. About the only concession to creature comfort provided for free are two new and very comfortable bucket seats. You sit high in these, and it takes a while to get used to the open-air togetherness with surrounding traffic. When this is at high speed, such as on a crowded freeway, you never quite get used to it. Seat belts here are not so much a matter of accident protection, but a needed lifeline at all times.

The 81-inch-wheelbase Universal model is peppy enough in standard form with a 4-cylinder F-head engine that puts out 75 hp. With the optional 160-hp V-6 Buick powerplant, the configuration of our test car, the 90-mph highpoint on the big speedometer is not unattainable with the standard 3.92 axle. The Jeep people have labeled this combination "Dauntless," and when front drive is engaged, this mechanical bull will plow through anything that doesn't overcrowd the 8-inch ground clearance. It will climb any grade up to about 63%, and might do better if you could talk your passengers into sitting on the front fenders.

Stuffing the V-6 into a Jeep was an invigorator known to the off-road fraternity long before the factory in Toledo got around to officially engineering the installation. Being not much, if any, longer than the 4-banger it replaces, it fits neatly with adequate air pockets for servicing. Very early production routed the exhaust pipe below the transfer-case guard where the pipe was vulnerable to damage, but this was soon remedied with retrofit. Because of the lack of insulation, there is more of a pockety-pock sound from the engine at idle and low speed than in its native Buick, but it smooths out like a V-8 at anything over 1500 rpm.

We do feel that something could be done about the need for a boarding-house reach to engage the front-drive mechanism. High range (pull back) may be engaged at road speed, but to do so, one must lose sight of the road momentarily. For low range, of course, the vehicle must be brought to almost a complete stop, where the diverted attention doesn't matter.

We learned once again, too, that the engagement must be complete or, under load, the drive will snap into neutral, which can cause some hairy moments on a real steep hill. The 4wd, of course, should be restricted to snow, mud or

Cat-like V-6 Universal Jeep will crest grades up to 63% with ease, but floppy mirror nearly clipped some oncoming cars.

Powerful heater, with controls under speedometer, helped temper the lack of a roof. Windshield can be folded for more breeze.

As Jeep rodeo fans have long known, Buick V-6 is a natural fit with no cutting necessary. Alternator puts out 35 amps.

other soft terrain. In it, under the proper circumstances, you get the feeling that you can go anywhere. The car kind of claws at uneven surfaces one wheel at a time in an undulating fashion that causes noticeable chassis movement.

Any Jeep-type vehicle, of necessity, is a little top-heavy. They are fine when climbing or descending longitudinally, but don't try tilting them too far. Should she start sliding slowly, get into low low and turn uphill. If she lets go abruptly, turn downhill in any gear. If all of this fails, bail out on the high side. Also remember that the Jeep was not designed to corner like a sports car. Its cam-and-lever steering is quick and has a desirable short radius for cross-country use, but the off-side front wheel can dig in and flip you.

A highly desirable accessory is either the Warn or Cutlass Powerlock front hub. When positioned for 2-wheel drive on the highway, these lock out the heavy front-end parts and gain by Jeep's own tests from 1 to 1½ mpg in economy. This soon pays back the $67.50 or $55 initial cost (plus installation), respectively. We also recommend investing in some form of roof and side curtains. They're cheaper than the wonder drugs needed to cure the respiratory ailments generated by uncovered Jeeps. Unfortunately, an overdrive is not yet available with the V-6 engine, and neither is the 4-speed transmission, which really isn't needed.

If we had our druthers, we'd like to see the gear shift mounted on the column which, in turn, would enable crooking the transfer-case lever over towards the driver where it could be more easily reached. Another item which bemuses us is the five feet or so of rubber tubing to the windshield wipers. You tend to grab at it when you climb in, and it is not strong enough for this purpose. The experimentally minded will find it possible to light a cigarette with the suction in the line, but this isn't too practical, either. In other words, now that Jeep has got its wipers motorized, let's electrify them.

The new cowl-hinged accelerator pedal is big and rubber-coated so your foot doesn't bounce off it in rough terrain. The other two pedals, too, are handily placed. We would like to see, though, some form of gritty stuff sprayed on the bare metal floors like those strips they use to keep you from slipping in motel bathtubs. That Jeep floor, as it stands, can get just as slippery as any bathtub when it's wet. Lastly, don't bother with that last gallon of gas in the tank. After baking in the sun a bit, a full tank emits a little geyser of fuel through the vent until equilibrium is restored to its innards.

— *Don MacDonald*

Sturdy bumper protects the steering mechanism when there are small trees growing in the road. The Jeep is real family fun.

Standard trailer hitch sometimes scrapes but it is too tough to bend. Don't forget the spare tire out there when parking.

JEEP UNIVERSAL

4-passenger, 4-wheel-drive utility vehicle

SPECIFICATIONS FROM MANUFACTURER

ENGINE IN TEST CAR: Ohv V-6
- Bore and stroke: 3.75 x 3.4 ins.
- Displacement: 225 cu. ins.
- Advertised horsepower: 160 @ 4400 rpm
- Max. torque: 235 lbs.-ft. @ 2400 rpm
- Compression ratio: 9.0:1
- Carburetion: 1 2-bbl.

TRANSMISSION TYPE & FINAL DRIVE RATIO: 3-speed manual, floor-mounted lever. 3.92:1 rear-axle ratio, 4.88 with overdrive

SUSPENSION: Variable-rate leaf springs, with hydraulic shock absorbers at each wheel

STEERING: Cam and lever
- Turning diameter: 35.9 ft., curb to curb
- Turns lock to lock: 2.58

WHEELS: Steel disc, 16-in. dia.

TIRES: 6.00 x 16, 4-ply-rated rayon

BRAKES: Hydraulic internal-expansion, duo-servo floating shoe
- Diameter of drum: front, 9 ins.; rear, 9 ins.

SERVICE:
- Type of fuel recommended: Regular
- Fuel capacity: 10½ gals.
- Oil capacity: 4 qts.; with filter: 5 qts.
- Shortest lubrication interval: 1000 mi.
- Oil- and filter-change interval: 2000 mi.

BODY & FRAME: Ladder-type frame with steel side members
- Wheelbase: 81.0 ins.
- Track: front, 48.44 ins.; rear, 48.44 ins.
- Overall: length, 138.16 ins.; width, 71.75 ins.; height, 69.5 ins.
- Min. ground clearance: 8.0 ins.
- Usable trunk capacity: not applicable
- Curb weight: 3750 lbs.

ACCESSORY PRICE LIST

*Right side seat	$ 51.00
Rear seat	78.25
Convertible top (installed)	165.00
Power winch (installed)	360.00
Limited-slip differential (rear only)	45.15
*Warn hubs (installed)	77.50
Cutlass powerlock hubs	55.00
Heavy-duty clutch	7.71
*Heater	84.00
AM radio	61.00
Steel cab	475.00
Whitewall tires	12.70
Outside-mounted gas cans (each)	6.50
Outside carrying racks (each)	3.00

*On test car

MANUFACTURER'S SUGGESTED LIST PRICE: $2880.11 (incl. taxes, safety equip't & PCV device)

PRICE OF CAR TESTED: $3092.11 (incl. excise tax, delivery & get-ready charges, but not local tax & license)

MANUFACTURER'S WARRANTY: 12,000 miles and/or 12 months

The metallic cavalry we have assembled here represents the newest wave in middle-class hip. A few years back the only guy who bought himself an off-the-road vehicle was, most likely, an oil field rigger, a forest ranger, a prospector, a Minute Man, a white hunter, or a social outcast who was just plain nuts about shunning not only pikes but every other form of paved road as well. Nowadays, it seems like every red-blooded American suburbanite wants a Jeep or one of its many offspring.

If it hasn't already happened on your block, one of these bright days you can expect a call from some Captain Virility of the Split-Level Set, inviting you over to take a look at his newest automotive acquisition. You'll rush right over, expecting to see a sleek new Lamborghini or, at the very least, a 427 Sting Ray. But what you'll find is one of these incredible monsters standing there in all its high, slab-sided glory. The suspension will be sticking out from the undercarriage, the tops of the fenders will be only slightly below your breastbone, and there'll be a cab towering so high you figure you'll get a nosebleed if you ever have to go for a ride—provided, of course, that your atrophied muscles are strong enough to vault you into the seat.

Meanwhile, old Captain Virility scrambles out of the cab and launches into a frenzied rhapsody about how *practical,* how tough, how well-made, how *honest* his new vehicle is. It's the medium he alone has discovered to transport him "back to nature." No more deceiving himself with a $5000 foreign sports car that he can't enjoy because of the traffic, and the fuzz, and the money it costs to get it serviced; from now on it's back to fundamental values—sea, sand, sky, rocks, trees—and there ain't nothin' can stop him!

Come on, neighbor. Every beach within 200 miles is now restricted to specially-authorized beach buggies, and there's a mile-long waiting list to get one of the coveted permits. If Captain Virility tries to use his proud new possession up in the mountains, he's more than likely to come home with a load of buckshot in his tail, courtesy of the farmer who owns the land he was trespassing on.

You know all this . . . and so does he. But *dammit,* you still can't help admire him, his rugged individualism—you're a little jealous of his new, Hemingway ap-

GET OFF THE ROAD!

We try several samples of the automotive world's all-purpose elixir for whatever might ail you...and they all work.

PHOTOGRAPHY: GARY RENAUD

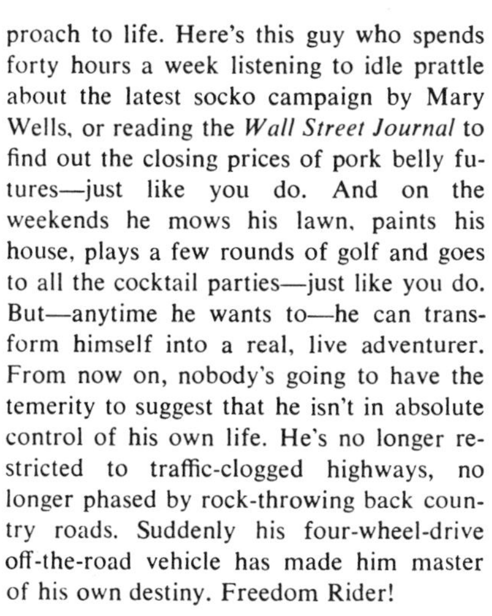

proach to life. Here's this guy who spends forty hours a week listening to idle prattle about the latest socko campaign by Mary Wells, or reading the *Wall Street Journal* to find out the closing prices of pork belly futures—just like you do. And on the weekends he mows his lawn, paints his house, plays a few rounds of golf and goes to all the cocktail parties—just like you do. But—anytime he wants to—he can transform himself into a real, live adventurer. From now on, nobody's going to have the temerity to suggest that he isn't in absolute control of his own life. He's no longer restricted to traffic-clogged highways, no longer phased by rock-throwing back country roads. Suddenly his four-wheel-drive off-the-road vehicle has made him master of his own destiny. Freedom Rider!

It really doesn't matter that the damn thing's transfer case will probably rust away from disuse, and that the power-winch securely bolted to the front bumper will only be used to haul helpless saplings out of the backyard. When friend Virility goes roaring and bucking into town, even if it's just for another case of Beefeaters, poor slobs like you are bound to think wistfully of all the good times he *can* have in that lumbering little truck.

And, no matter how many niggling laws restrict its use, a four-wheel-drive vehicle is fun. Big fun. We spent a couple of weeks tearing up sand and sod around Long Island beaches and the hills behind Bridgehampton Race Circuit with five such vehicles: a long-wheelbase Land Rover, a Toyota Land Cruiser, an International Scout, a Jeep Universal, and a Ford Bronco. And we all wish we could do it more often. (Originally, we had planned to include another vehicle, the Datsun Patrol, but miffed at our treatment of their economy sedan, the RL-411 (*C/D*, May), Datsun refuses to submit any more of their vehicles for our evaluation.)

When this test was first proposed we had assumed that all four-wheel-drive vehicles are pretty much alike. How wrong we were. Off-the-road vehicles remain one of the few products for which each manufacturer has its own concept of what constitutes the ideal. Perhaps nowhere is the difference so apparent as in the prices of the five vehicles we tested. Rather than specify exactly what we wanted, we asked each of the companies to provide us with a vehicle that, in their opinion, represented the best compromise between second-car practicality and off-the-road fun. Rover was the only one to provide us with a long-wheelbase version (probably because their big six-cylinder engine is only available in the long-wheelbase model). Kaiser, on the other hand, went to the other extreme and provided us with a vitamin-packed V-6 in their short-wheelbase version of the ubiquitous Jeep Universal. On two points, at least, all five manufacturers agreed; all the cars came through with metal hardtops and heater/defroster units. The cars which were most comfortable in the over-the-road portion of our test, the Ford Bronco and the Rover, both came equipped with radios, while the best off-the-road models, the Jeep and the Rover (again), also came with power winches. The Toyota, well-placed in both categories and probably the best value for the money, had neither a radio nor a winch.

Because the vehicles we tested were equipped with widely differing amounts of extra-cost options, it is important to note in the specifications table that the prices are "as tested," and not base prices for each model. Other specifications vary accordingly, and are not intended as a source of direct comparison. Our intention is to present some basic information and our impressions of typical examples from each of the manufacturers.

The vast differences in fittings, ride comfort and performance reflect the individual manufacturer's design emphasis rather than the foibles of a particular version. For instance, the medium-priced Jeep V-6 was far and away the most spartan, being almost devoid of instrumentation and totally lacking in sound-deadening insulation, but it also had the most comfortable seats of the bunch. At the other extreme was the Land Rover, which had the most comprehensive dashboard and loads of nifty little convenience gadgets like swing-up steps and four doors instead of just two, but its seats were not nearly as comfortable as the Jeep's. The Ford Bronco was the smoothest riding, most softly sprung member of the group, and it was the only one equipped with a coil spring suspension instead of semi-elliptic leaf springs on all four wheels. It had obviously been designed primarily for over-the-road comfort and *occasional* off-the-road use. Had it not been for the pseudo-Mustang bucket seats the Bronco would have been, far and away, the most comfortable car. Unfortunately, the padding around the edges of the Bronco's seats is so thick that your back is supported only at the shoulder blades—the rest of you caves into an uncomfortable hunchbacked position. The Toyota had the harshest suspension and was the roughest riding of the group, but its very stiff spring rates helped make it an outstanding off-the-road performer.

In terms of acceleration, our little Jeep left the rest of the field panting in its wake. But its narrow spring leaves had so much lateral compliance that it would shift disconcertingly from side to side under any kind of side load. This, plus a chronically grabbing brake, made everyone wary of driving the little stormer in heavy traffic.

Whether a compromise between over-the-road and off-the-road usage is desirable turned out to be a different matter. The Scout had no outstanding attributes because it—more than any of the others—was designed as a compromise. The result was that no one felt very strongly about it one way or the other. Most automotive devices have some kind of personality; the Scout didn't. It was like a washing machine—a solid, utilitarian appliance that gets the job done largely unnoticed.

All of the cars were capable of keeping up with the incredible demands of driving on the Long Island Expressway, where one minute you're slogging along at four mph and the next you're caught up in a swarming phalanx of NASCAR racers who think nothing of drafting each other at 85 mph. The weakest member of our convoy was the Scout. Even though it was equipped with International's new V-8 engine, it simply lacked the acceleration to keep up. (In fairness, we should mention that this Scout was fresh off the assembly line with very few miles on it when we tested it.)

Except for the Land Rover, which had a four-speed transmission, all our test vehicles were equipped with three-speeds. None was what you would call slick shifting, and only the Bronco had a synchronized first gear (first *and* second on the four-speed Rover were unsynchronized). One fault common to all the cars was gear spacing. First and second gears were inevitably low ratio ranges, designed for maximum power application, with the high cruising gear a country mile away. This held true even for the four-speed Rover, with first being a sort of "underdrive" and second and third acting much the same as the lower two gears on the other vehicles' three-speeds.

Noise level in these cars was universally atrocious. The Ford Bronco—the most Detroit-ized of our test group—was the quietest, with the Scout a close second. The remaining three—Rover, Toyota and Jeep—are in a class by themselves. Suffice it to say that conversation is effectively drowned out, and that even thought pro-

Ford Bronco

International Scout

Jeep Universal

Land Rover

Toyota Land Cruiser

cesses can become confused as a result of the roaring and rattling all around you.

While none of these vehicles is in line for an award as the "world's most commodious station wagon," their off-the-road performance makes up for what they lack on the pavement. We began our off-the-road testing at the Bridgehampton Race Circuit on the end of Long Island. This windswept course is located in the midst of high, sandy dunes and proved to be an ideal testing ground for these vehicles. When we wanted loose sand it was available; as was hard sand, steep grades, thick underbrush and all the rest of the impossible conditions that a standard two-wheel drive vehicle can't handle. So we descended on Bridgehampton one bright morning and we came away different people—all of us. When our convoy was finally grouped around the administration building, our photographer mentioned that he'd like all of us to go out and search for a dramatic slope on which he could position the vehicles for a group shot. *Roar! Roar! Roar! Roar! Roar!* All five cars shot off in four-wheel-drive to find an appropriate location.

Dust clouds trailed each of the cars as they rumbled from dune to dune in search of the perfect setting. Spontaneous races broke out everywhere and it wasn't long before the photographer realized that no one was really interested in helping him out—we all just wanted to find out for ourselves what this off-the-road hang-up is all about.

It took nearly 45 minutes to get us regrouped and beaten into submission, and another 15 minutes before the beleaguered photographer found the spot he wanted. Finally, all five cars were staged on the side of THE hill. For another 15 minutes we sat patiently still while the cars were carefully (and somewhat precariously) positioned. As we stood there, waiting for the shot to be taken, challenges were hurled about like insults in a nightclub: "My Jeep will take that Rover up any hill you want to name," "The Land Cruiser will kill you both" and on and on.

When the photographer unwittingly cooperated by saying "Okay, I'm finished here. Now I'd like to get some running shots of the cars going over rough terrain," it was all over. He had given us the justification we needed for what we had been plotting all along.

The scene that followed was a Mack Sennett version of Le Mans. The drivers sprinted to their cars, and, within seconds, all five were fired up and roaring helter-skelter over every dune in sight.

It seemed that everyone felt it necessary to challenge the Land Rover, which was in the capable hands of our Technical Editor. Soon it was apparent that the only other cars that stood a chance were the Jeep and the Toyota. But, frantic as their efforts might be, the stately Land Rover couldn't be topped. The whole thing came to a halt when the Jeep, after nearly beating the

Rover up a particularly soft dune, got hung up on top of a hummock and had to be ignominiously pulled off with its winch.

All the off-the-road vehicles proved their worth in this spontaneous test procedure. The only one that was constantly left behind was the International Scout, whose engine didn't have the pulling power and kept wheezing to a halt midway up the steep dunes.

On the next day we trekked down to the deserted beaches to see if there were any marked differences on the long level stretches of very soft sand. There were. Our Toyota, which had been such a challenger at Bridgehampton, suddenly couldn't cut it. Not being what you would call a lightweight, and—because we had decided that we wanted to evaluate these cars as both off-the-road and over-the-road vehicles in the same trim—we hadn't bothered to reduce the pressure in any of the tires. *Scrunch.* The short-wheelbase Toyota bogged down. It simply sank into the sand and every time we stepped on the gas, its powerful engine would just dig us in more deeply. So out came the winch again—this time the one on the Rover. Even with their tires fully pumped up, the rest of the vehicles were able to make it through the hub-deep sand, although none but the Jeep, because of its light weight and fat tires, inspired any overwhelming confidence that you could, invariably, pull yourself out of any predicament you might get into.

Except for the International Scout, every one of these vehicles had one outstanding point. For the Jeep, it was its brute power. For the Bronco, its over-the-road comfort. For the Toyota, its outstanding performance in everything except soft sand. For the Rover, it was the ease with which it tackled any obstacle. But each vehicle except the Scout, had its faults as well. The Jeep was perched on an uncertain suspension. The Toyota was rough riding. The Bronco wasn't really designed for sustained use in rough terrain. And the Rover we tested was too expensive for most people in the market for a second car.

As we said at the outset, much of the recent demand for off-the-road vehicles comes from people who don't really need them, people who simply want something that will allow them to escape from the confines of their lives and the restrictions of a road map. After driving these cars for a couple of weeks, we can understand that philosophy. It's a great feeling to get out on an unmarked hunk of land and raise a whole lot of hell. So do yourself a favor. Get off to the outback and find out what it's all about. Go wherever you damn well please! It's guaranteed to soothe the mind, enliven the spirit, cure a multitude of nine-to-five maladies and alleviate irregularity. And there hasn't been anything like that for the last fifty years, except maybe Excedrin, which isn't nearly as much fun. **C/D**

OFF-THE-ROAD Specifications

	Ford Bronco	International Scout	Jeep Universal	Land Rover	Toyota Land Cruiser
Wheelbase	92.0 in	100.0 in	81.0 in	109.0 in	90.0 in
Track: F	57.4 in	56.1 in	48.5 in	51.5 in	55.3 in
R	57.4 in	55.7 in	48.5 in	51.5 in	55.1 in
Ground clearance	7.8 in	7.6 in	8.0 in	9.8 in	7.9 in
Weight	3165 lbs	3615 lbs	2274 lbs	3912 lbs	3470 lbs
Turning circle	33.5 ft	44.2 ft	40.3 ft	52.5 ft	36. ft
Engine:					
Type	In-line 6	V-8	V-6	In-line 6	In-line 6
Displ.	170 cu in	266 cu in	225 cu in	160 cu in	237 cu in
Power	105 hp	155 hp	160 hp	123 hp	134 hp
0-60 Time	19.4 secs.	20.5 secs.	10.8 secs.	18.5 secs.	16.9 secs.
Price (as tested)	$2922	$3491	$3310	$4950	$3181

Land Rover has full instrumentation and ventilation flaps beneath the windshield.

Jeep's instrumentation consists of a speedometer. For fresh air you open a window.

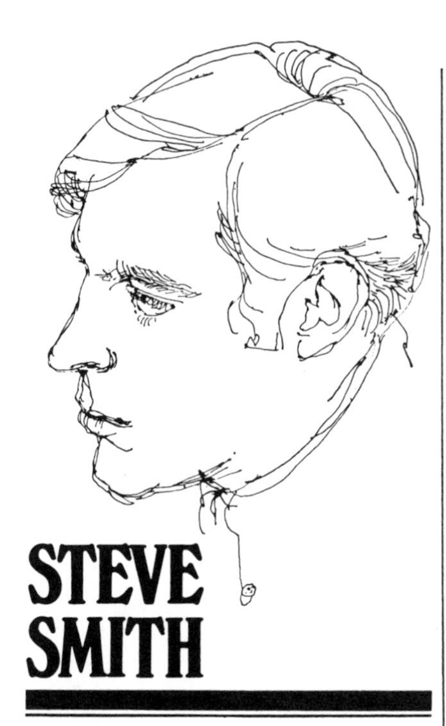

STEVE SMITH

I'm not much of a classic car buff. A vintage car, to me, is any car built before I went to high school, and a veteran car is anything built before World War II. I never went through a hot rod phase when I was young—it happened the other way around—first the exotica, only now the salt of the earth. The first car I ever really got exercised about was the Mercedes-Benz 300 SL coupe they raced in the Mexican Road Race. The one with the bars in front of the windshield, because a buzzard had crashed through the windshield of one of the cars the year before. You could keep your necker's knobs and Ardun heads, man, I promised myself that the first car I'd ever own would have buzzard bars.

Maybe it was just as well that I didn't put the bars on my first car—a Jeep, which would have looked pretty silly with buzzard bars on it anyway. Particularly since I drove it around with the windshield folded flat on the hood, "combat style," or so I had read.

It happened, in due time, that a friend of the family, a lady of my parent's generation, borrowed the Jeep, went for a ride, missed a turn on an icy road, and planted the nose of the Jeep right square in the middle of a tree. I was furious. I was indignant. I had spent hours practicing double-clutching into four-wheel-drive (at touring speeds, please note) at the slightest sign of ice--glare, black or otherwise. The lady, I noticed with grim satisfaction, was in two-wheel-drive when she'd crashed. The insurance company wrote it off, but we bought it back from the wrecking yard and had it fixed up. It was never the same after that, though.

The Jeep had originally been built for the Navy, and that stood it in good stead during one hurricane I remember. The sea rolled back and roared and flooded the lowlands. The beach residents were being evacuated. A girl I knew lived with her parents, and they refused to evacuate. They were going down with the house, as it were. When the water level reached the bottom floor of the house, they called me and begged me to rescue them. The Civil Defense people refused to go near the house, and the area was closed to any and all private rescue attempts. Could I get through? Could I get through! I put on all the white clothing I could find, borrowed a swabbies' cap from my sister (who, younger than I, affected such clothing) and drove off to the embattlements. At the CD checkpoint, I somehow managed to convince them that I had special clearance from the Department of the Navy. The clincher was the mobile radio set-up I had installed in the rear seat with a whip antenna that just wouldn't quit. I waved a hastily forged pass, stuffed the Jeep into first, and drove through the lines. I thought I'd never make it. In places, the water would come in over the door sills. The wheels would bog down, it was pitch black. I finally reached the house. Out front, there was a taxi. In the taxi was the family I had risked life and high water to save. They waved. The taxi drove off smartly, shouldering the water imperiously aside. Humiliated in front of my girl. I sat there with my sister's silly little hat perched on the top of my head and my laughable whip antenna waving around in the dark and I thought about killing myself right then and there.

Time heals all wounds. Soon I had myself convinced that I was not only the world's all-time greatest Jeep driver, but also holder of the Absolute Land Speed Record, Jeep Division. I didn't have the faintest idea of how to hop up that noisy little four-cylinder engine (the "spark intensifier" I'd paid $1.98 plus postage for didn't seem to do a thing for it), so I set about my record attempt with the oldest speed-tuning device known to man—gravity. There is this four-mile downhill stretch up in Connecticut, near Lime Rock, and I never—to this day—have seen a cop patrolling it. Roll bars hadn't happened yet, so the Jeep was made a bastion of safety by the installation of a seat belt. Anchorage points for belts hadn't happened yet, either, so I took some canvas webbing, ran it under the seat—under the gas tank, actually, and cinched it around my waist. If the Jeep had ever turned over, I either would have been flung into oblivion strapped to a gas tank or crushed underneath the Jeep like a bug. Feeling all snug and secure because of my wise-beyond-my-years safety precautions, my friend and I set off down the four-mile hill, from a 60 mph flying start. We were hip to aerodynamics, and not only removed (not just folded) the windshield, special for this event, but also spent much of the descent huddled as low as we could possibly get, the bills of our red Holden Caulfield hunting caps turned around out of the wind. For one fleeting moment—the engine revving insanely, the wind flailing madly, the Jeep leaping and bucking over what was really a pretty smooth stretch of road—for one moment, the speedometer needle crept beyond the last pair of digits on the dial—80 mph. Later, we both agreed that it had actually read as high as 84 mph, indicated (or, rather, extrapolated), and maybe even 85. We were quite clear on that point, and billed ourselves as World Speed Record holders for some years afterwards.

Meanwhile, I had discovered sports car racing and instantly concluded that it would prove an irresistible lure to girls. "Hey, how about you coming to the sports car races with me up at Harewood this weekend?" Harewood would sound, to her, like it was right around the next bend in the road. Actually, Harewood was in Canada, and Canada was about 500 miles away. I discovered that girls, on the whole, don't like 1000-mile jaunts in Jeeps, at least not with the windshield folded, combat style. We would leave in the small hours of Sunday morning. No matter how fast or how slow I would drive, we would always average exactly 42 mph (just as, later on, when I attempted engine tuning on a chassis dyno, I would always extract precisely 67 horsepower from every engine I ever laid a wrench on, from a Hemi to a VW). We would arrive in an absolute stupor from being wind-whipped for 10 hours. We couldn't hear a thing. We had no tactile sensations in our faces, hands and behinds. Exhausted, we would doze off (about the time George Arents' Siata passed Bill Sadler's TR-3), huddled under a tarp at the base of an abandoned concrete bunker—it always rained. Then we'd drive all the way home, fighting off sleep by driving fast enough to stay scared. On the whole, girls didn't much care for going to the races in my Jeep. So I decided that I had to become a racer myself, and fly to the races in a chartered airplane, like the other amateur drivers of the day, but I obviously wasn't going to get a berth on the Cunningham team (everything was "Ecurie" something or other in those days, but I don't think Briggs ever succumbed) until I learned the tricks of the trade. After a very nasty business with a local cop, I decided that practice on normal public roads was out. I eventually found a set of sandy roads in the pine barrens that connected to make a challenging (to me) 2.1-mile circuit. Soon I learned how to make a car spin out. By all that's holy, I should have learned how to overturn a car in sand (complete with my deadly safety belt), but, as usual, I survived. Some time later, I almost didn't; falling off a mountain while rock climbing and shattering both myself and the Mountaineer's Club fall picnic. The Jeep was, by that time, sold to a nice family from Nantucket, and the last I heard—about six years ago—it was still going strong. ●

UNI-TRAC IS A JEEP.

IS A JEEP?

IS A JEEP!

Think you've seen every possible gimmick in modifying a Jeep? Well, unless you have been out to Brian Chuchua's 4wd Center in Fullerton, California lately, then pass on this question. Because the fellow who said Chuchua would try anything was right. After taking a ride in his latest innovation, nobody is able to say whether he has built a Jeep that acts like a tank . . . or a tank that acts like a Jeep.

Anything you decide is all right for it's a happy marriage, even though mixed unions seldom work. Called a Uni-Trac by its makers, the outfit consists of two steel tracks, four hub adapters, two steering levers and the hardware to install the unit.

The beauty of this invention is that it is really a temporary adaptation. In a minimum of time (about one hour for a person with average mechanical ability) the rig can be re-converted back to its original form.

FOUR WHEELER did not make a major test of the Uni-Trac, so this report is necessarily a little brief. But then, only a short acquaintance is necessary to see the potential of the Uni-Trac in extreme applications. The test outfit was a V-6 powered CJ-5 with the tracked goodies installed. Since the Uni-Trac's maximum recommended speed is 15 mph, the Jeep's first two compound gear ratios worked the best.

With the test track installed, the CJ walked over obstacles and crevices that would have ham strung any conventional rig. To an experienced off-road driver it was obvious that exceptionally soft soil and even snow should pose little or no problems at all.

In fact, the tracked-Jeep is so mobile that it might tend to give the driver the confidence of a "cat" driver. A good axiom to be followed would be to be extremely cautious on side slopes where lateral slippage could occur and lead to trouble. The track-layer is so good it will put you there at the slightest urging.

One of the major reasons for this mobility is not hard to track down. The Uni-Trac equipped Jeep has extremely high flotation displacing only 3.5 pounds of ground pressure, which is considerably less than the biggest flotation tires on a stock Jeep.

Regular operating features are not unlike the typical tracked tractor in that the two levers positioned between the front seats when actuated pivot the rig. It is possible for a Uni-Trac rig to completely turn within its own length.

Construction of the Uni-Trac is steel and all cast components are of ductile iron. All bearings are lifetime lubricated.

The uses for the Uni-Trac are innumerable and limited only by the imagination and needs of a four wheeler. The fully tracked rig can be put to the following uses: cultivating, snaking timber, blading, pulling a sheep foot for compaction, utility rig at ski resorts or a ready packer for the nimrod in hunting country.

While no one is going to suggest that four wheelers are going to use the Uni-Trac for general off-road trips, owning one does not tie up the Jeep for any length of time. Simply unbolt the tracks and put the wheels back on and you are in business again. For the fellow who has terrain problems that even a good set of flotation tires can't solve it is going to be the answer.

Kaiser Jeep
JEEP UNIVERSAL

ENGINE CAPACITY 134.20 cu in, 2,199.13 cu cm
FUEL CONSUMPTION 25.7 m/imp gal, 21.4 m/US gal, 11 l × 100 km
SEATS 5 - 6 **MAX SPEED** 78 mph, 125.6 km/h
PRICE —

ENGINE front, 4 stroke; cylinders: 4, vertical, in line; bore and stroke: 3.12 × 4.37 in, 79.2 × 111 mm; engine capacity: 134.20 cu in, 2,199.13 cu cm; compression ratio: 7.4; max power (SAE): 75 hp at 4,000 rpm; max torque (SAE): 114 lb ft, 15.7 kg m at 2,000 rpm; max engine rpm: 4,600; specific power: 34.1 hp/l; cylinder block: cast iron; cylinder head: cast iron; crankshaft bearings: 3; valves: 2 per cylinder, overhead, in line, push-rods and rockers; camshafts: 1, side; lubrication: rotary pump, filter on by-pass; lubricating system capacity: 8.27 imp pt, 10 US pt, 4.7 l; carburation: 1 Carter YF 938 SD downdraught single barrel carburettor; fuel feed: mechanical pump; cooling system: water; cooling system capacity: 20.06 imp pt, 24 US pt, 11.4 l.

TRANSMISSION driving wheels: front (automatically engaged with transfer box low ratio) and rear; clutch: single dry plate; gearbox: mechanical; gears: 3 with high and low ratios + reverse; synchromesh gears: II and III; gearbox ratios: I 3.339 (low 5.80), II 1.551 (low 4.01), III 1 (low 2.46), rev 3.798 (low 6.26); gear and low ratio levers: steering column; final drive: hypoid bevel; axle ratio: 4.270.

CHASSIS ladder frame, lateral members; front suspension: rigid axle, semi-elliptic leafsprings, telescopic dampers; rear suspension: rigid axle, semi-elliptic leafsprings, telescopic dampers.

STEERING cam and peg; turns of steering wheel lock to lock: 2.58.

BRAKES drum, 2 front leading shoes; lining area: total 102.65 sq in, 662.09 sq cm

ELECTRICAL EQUIPMENT voltage: 12 V; battery: 50 Ah; generator type: alternator, 35 Ah; headlamps: 2.

DIMENSIONS AND WEIGHT wheel base: 81 in, 2,057 mm; front track: 48.45 in, 1,231 mm; rear track: 48.45 in, 1,231 mm; overall length: 138.15 in, 3,509 mm: overall width: 71.75 in, 1,822 mm; overall height: 69.50 in, 1,765 mm; ground clearance: 8 in, 203 mm; dry weight: 2,278 lb, 1,033 kg; turning circle (between walls): 37 ft, 11.3 m; tyres: 6.00 × 16; fuel tank capacity: 8.8 imp gal, 10.5 US gal, 40 l.

BODY estate car/station wagon; doors: 4 + 1; seats: 5 - 6; front seats: separate.

PERFORMANCE max speeds: 27 mph, 43.5 km/h in 1st gear; 57 mph, 91.8 km/h in 2nd gear; 78 mph, 125.6 km/h in 3rd gear; power-weight ratio: 30.4 lb/hp, 13.8 kg/hp; carrying capacity: 1,058 lb, 480 kg; speed in direct drive at 1,000 rpm: 19.3 mph, 31.1 km/h.

PRACTICAL INSTRUCTIONS fuel: 90 oct petrol; engine sump oil: 6.69 imp pt, 8 US pt, 3.8 l, SAE 20, change every 3,000 miles, 4,800 km; gearbox oil: 2.46 imp pt, 3 US pt, 1.4 l, SAE 90, change every 12,000 miles, 19,300 km; final drive oil: 2.11 imp pt, 2.50 US pt, 1.2 l, SAE 90, change every 6,000 miles, 9,700 km; greasing: every 1,000-6,000 miles, 1,600-9,700 km, 33 points; tappet clearances: inlet 0.018 in, 0.46 mm, exhaust 0.016 in, 0.41 mm; valve timing: inlet opens 9° before tdc and closes 50° after bdc, exhaust opens 47° before bdc and closes 12° after tdc; normal tyre pressure: front 26 psi, 1.8 atm, rear 28 psi, 2 atm.

160 hp V6 engine

VARIATIONS AND OPTIONAL ACCESSORIES 6.9 compression ratio; 7.00 × 16 tyres; 4-speed mechanical gearbox (I 6.398, II 3.092, III 1.686, IV 1, rev 7.820); engine 7.35 × 15 tyres, total area rubbed by linings 174 sq in, 1,122.30 sq cm, wheel base 101 in, 2,565 mm, overall length 158.15 in, 4,017 mm, overall height 68.25 in, 1,733 mm, turning circle (between walls) 43 ft, 13.1 m; Perkins Diesel engine, capacity 192.40 cu in, 3,152.86 cu cm, bore and stroke 3.50 × 5 in, 88.9 × 127 mm, max power (SAE) 60 hp at 3,000 rpm, max torque (SAE) 143 lb ft, 19.7 kg m at 1,350 rpm, 16.5 compression ratio, 19 hp/l specific power; engine 6 cylinders Vee-slanted at 90°, capacity 225 cu in, 3,687.07 cu cm, bore and stroke 3.75 × 3.40 in, 95.2 × 86.4 mm, max power (SAE) 160 hp at 4,200 rpm, max torque (SAE) 235 lb ft, 32.4 kg m at 2,400 rpm, max engine rpm 4,500, 9 compression ratio, 43.4 hp/l specific power, hydraulic tappets, 3-speed mechanical gearbox (I 2.790, II 1.680, III 1, rev 3.790), 3.730 axle ratio, total area rubbed by linings 174 sq in, 1,122.30 sq cm, 7.35 × 15 tyres, dry weight 3,200 lb, 1,451 kg, valve timing 24° 81° 72° 43°, speed in direct drive at 1,000 rpm 22.1 mph, 35.6 km/h, max speeds (I) 36 mph, 58 km/h, (II) 59 mph, 95 km/h, (III) 90 mph, 144.9 km/h, fuel consumption 20.2 m/imp gal, 16.8 m/US gal, 14 l × 100 km ■ Jeep Tuxedo Park Mark IV, only with V6 engine ■ Jeepster Convertible.

JEEP

Certainly the biggest news item of 1969 in the 4-wheel industry was American Motors buying the Jeep line from Kaiser Industries. The term "jeep" is now used almost universally as a type designation for any short-wheelbased 4-wheel-drive vehicle, but is actually a tradename of American Motors at present. The original Jeeps were built by the Willys company early in World War 2 for the U.S. Army. During the war, some were made by Ford on contract to Willys. Kaiser eventually bought out Willys, along with the name, which originated in the Army's abbreviation of the vehicle's official designation: General Purpose. It was easier to call it a "G. P.," and even easier to call it a "Jeep."

The Jeep line manufactured today offers one of the widest selections of chassis, bodies and engines in the 4-wheel-drive field. Smallest and most Jeep-like in a World War 2 sense is the Universal line, with two wheelbases, two engines, and many variations. The Jeepster line is a bit more sophisticated (and more comfortable), with one wheelbase, two engines, and four basic body styles: roadster, convertible, station wagon and pickup. The Jeep Gladiator pickup comes in three wheelbases, two engines and four bodies. Finally, the Jeep Wagoneer is a posh 4-wheel-drive station wagon in one wheelbase, two engines, and in Standard or Custom configurations. With this range of variations, and prices starting at around $2900 for the Universal up to about $4800 for the Custom Wagoneer, if you can't find a Jeep model that suits your particular needs, you might as well forget 4-wheel drive. About the only thing you'll find anywhere else that Jeep doesn't have is a V-8 engine for the smaller Universal and Jeepster line. Jeep's biggest engine for these lines is the ex-Buick V-6, with 155 hp.

As we mentioned, the Universal is the Jeep in its most basic form. There are three current variations: the 2-wheel-drive DJ5 and the 4-wheel-drive CJ5 with 81-inch wheelbase, and the 4-wheel-drive CJ6 with 101-inch wheelbase. Incidentally, the DJ5 is the only 2-wheel-drive Jeep manufactured. Purely functional machines, the CJ5 and CJ6 have few frills, although the Jeep people have begun to come up with an interesting group of add-on options.

The 1969 Baja 1000 provided a demonstration of the overall ruggedness of the Universal Jeep. Bob Seivert and Dan Widner drove their 1951 military-surplus CJ3A Jeep to Baja from Colorado Springs, Colo. As Seivert had replaced the original 4-cylinder engine with the V-6 (which was not an option in 1951), the car had to run in the modified or non-production class, rather than with the current production models. This put them in the same race with the Chevy-powered Baja Boot driven by Steve McQueen, Con-Ferr's experimental car, a Chevy-powered Mini-Boot, a bunch of Chevotas (Toyota Land Cruisers with 327-Chevy engines) and several modified Ford Broncos. Everyone snickered when they saw the 18-year-old Jeep in the pits.

A day later there was something of a shocked silence as Seivert and Widner motored into La Paz in 23 hours, 36 minutes and 48 seconds, almost 5 hours ahead of the next car in the non-production 4-wheel-drive class! Amazingly enough, if the CJ3A had been allowed to run in the production 4-wheel-drive class, it still would have taken 2nd in that class. The winning Bronco of Minor and Hall made it in close to 3 hours less than the CJ3A, but the 2nd place production 4-wheel-drive (one of Brian Chuchua's Jeepsters) was 21 seconds slower.

Chuchua, whose crew prepared Jeep's "factory entry," had nine entered, with four Jeepsters, two 2-wheel-drive DJ6's, two 4-wheel-drive CJ6's and a Gladiator pickup. The 2-wheel-drives were unimpressive, since none made it to La Paz within the 48-hour time limit. In the production 4-wheel-drive class, Jeepsters finished 2nd and 3rd, almost 3 hours behind the winning Ford Bronco, with a CJ5 coming in 10th. None of the Jeeps in Chuchua's team ran in the non-production class.

Back to the Jeep Universal: Late in 1969, a "462" package became available for the CJ5, to be added to the Universal already equipped with the 160-hp V-6 engine, bucket seats and safety package. The "462" package includes a roll bar, a rear swing-out tire carrier, five red-striped H70x 15 Polyglas tubeless tires, heavy-duty oil pan and skidplate, electric oil gauge and ammeter, and stainless steel wheel covers.

2

Other factory-installed accessories include a rear seat with dual seat belts, tow bar, dash-mounted safety rail, heavy-duty frame, springs and shocks and a limited-slip rear end.

Although usually seen as an open, doorless roadster, there are also half and full soft tops, and half or full metal tops available, plus solid or cloth doors. Standard engine is a minimal-power 134-cubic-inch, 75-hp, 4-banger. It's extremely reliable and

1. Using mostly factory components, Brian Chuchua's fleet of prepared Jeeps have made their mark in racing.

2. Jeep with "462" package is the factory muscle car of the off-road world. Roll bar, H70x15 tires, gauges, and 160-hp V-6 mill give the buyer a head start in race preparation.

JEEP

frightfully uninteresting for anything but commercial use. The optional engine is the ex-Buick V-6, which Kaiser named the "Dauntless," at $210. This delivers 155 or 160 hp, depending on which brochure you read. It's plenty for any but very specialized off-road or closed-course racing.

As the Universal comes with a driver's seat only, you have to buy any additional seats to fit your particular needs. You can buy snowplows, winches, and all sorts of power takeoff accessories similar to those sold for the International Scout.

The normal transmission is a 3-speed on the inline-4 and a 4-speed on the V-6, with this last an option for the 4's. The 4-wheel-drive Universals come with five 6.00x16 4-ply all-service tube tires, or factory optional tires—five 8.55x15 4-ply Suburbanites (at less than $50 the set). As with just about all optional tires offered by 4-wheel-drive manufacturers, think of the largest available as being the smallest you should consider for off-road use, and not even worth mentioning for real competition.

A completely startling option for the Jeep Universal is the "Jeep Camper." It's made to fit the 81-inch-wheelbase CJ5 Universal, with the V-6 engine needed for power. It will sleep four people, and has as much floor space as most 10½-foot pickup Okie boxes. The gimmick is that it has its own set of two wheels, so it actually amounts to a trailer but—being rigidly mounted to the back of the Jeep—it is legally and physically a camper. It is complete with a butane stove, stainless steel sink, 20-gallon water tank and pressure system, marine-type toilet and holding tank . . . the whole bag. With the surefootedness of the 4-wheel-drive Universal, you can take the Jeep Camper almost anywhere, lower a couple of supports and drive out from under it, freeing the CJ5 for boondocking. Absolutely weird!

Options for the Camper include a 9000-BTU heater, Monomatic toilet, gas/electric refrigerator and interior gaslights. For the CJ5 you can buy a 4.88:1 axle ratio that is recommended with the Camper, a limited-slip rear end, free-wheeling front hubs, snap-in carpeting, a front-mounted winch and overdrive for freeway driving.

The Jeepster Commando line has an equally wide range of variations on a basic theme, but has smoother, less stark lines than the Universal. The Jeepster can be bought as an open roadster, a convertible, a pickup or a station wagon. Standard engine in all of these is the 4-banger, with the V-6 as a $210 option. With the V-6, it is quite possible to tow a trailer up to 3500 pounds in weight, and an optional General Motors Turbo Hydra-Matic can make it easier.

SPECIFICATIONS	
Wheelbase	101.0
Overall length	158.2
Width	71.75
Height	67.0
Front tread	48.5
Rear tread	48.5
Ground clearance	8.0
Box length—floor	54.0±
Box length—top	47.5±
Box width—floor	55.42
Box width—tailgate	36.0
Box depth	14.0
Max. gross vehicle wt.	3200

2

JEEP CJ-5

THE JEEP CJ-5 is the 1971 version of the World War II military Jeep that you could say actually started the trend toward the use of 4-wheel-drive vehicles for recreational purposes. Four-wheel-drive has been around for a long time—Spyker having used 4wd in 1902—but until World War II it was almost entirely restricted to heavy duty use as typified by the large motorized wagon-type vehicles built by the Four Wheel Drive Co. in the middle west. But with World War II, 4wd was applied to light, highly maneuverable small vehicles and that, more or less, is where we are today.

The name, "Jeep," as a matter of incidental interest came from E.C. Segar's comic strip, "Thimble Theatre—Starring Popeye," in 1936 wherein was introduced a small character named Eugene the Jeep, an interesting creature that could predict the future and allegedly only spoke the truth. In early 1940, the U.S. army was looking for a small, rugged vehicle for reconnaisance work and the Jeep's immediate predecessor was built by the American Bantam Co. on a prototype contract from the Army. The Willys-Overland Co. and Ford got into the act a little later and as it was the Willys design that proved best suited to the military purpose, it was their vehicle that was accepted for mass production in World War II. Ford was a second source for the military Jeep and before the war was over, over 300,000 Jeeps had been built by the two companies.

The military Jeep of WW II was basically a simple, rugged, go-anywhere machine. It had a 134.2-cu-in. L-head, 4-cyl engine that developed 60 horsepower at 4000 rpm and 105 lb-ft torque at 2000. There was a 2-speed transfer case, a 3-speed manual transmission with non-synchromesh first gear and the basic model weighed about 2450 lb.

The current specification of the CJ-5 is very similar. Same engine (but now with 75 horsepower instead of 60), same 3-speed gearbox and even the supplier of the axles and transfer case (Warner and Dana) are still on board.

JEEP CJ-5

PRICES

Basic list for CJ-5 Universal, open body, FOB Toledo: $2868

Standard equipment: 134-cu-in. 4-cyl engine, 3-spd manual transmission, oil bath air cleaner, driver seat only, 4PR 6.00x16 tires, 4wd

Other models: CJ-6 Universal ($2962) is same basic vehicle but with longer wheelbase (101 in. vs. 81).

Basic variations offered: open body, full fabric top, half fabric top, full metal top, half metal top.

Other prices for options are included in data below.

ENGINES

Standard engine .... inline ohv 4
Bore x stroke, in ....3.125 x 4.375
Displacement, cu in 134.2
Compression ratio ....7.1:1 or 6.3:1
Bhp @ rpm .... 75 @ 4000
Torque @ rpm, lb-ft .... 114 @ 2000
Type fuel required .... regular
Air cleaner type ....oil bath

Optional V-6 engine $211
Bore x stroke, in ....3.75 x 3.40
Displacement, cu in 225
Compression ratio 9.0:1
Bhp @ rpm .... 160 @ 4200
Torque @ rpm, lb-ft .... 235 @ 2400
Type fuel required .... regular
Air cleaner type ....oil bath

CHASSIS & BODY

Body/frame: ladder with X-members, steel body.

Brakes ..... 10 x 2-in. drums front & rear
Swept area, sq.in. 256
Power brakes ....not available

Steering type .... cam & lever
Steering ratio 17.9:1
Turning circle, ft 37.0
Power steering ....not available

Wheel size, std 16x5.5
Optional wheel sizes: 16x4.50E, 15x5.50K, 15x6K
Tire size, std 4pr 6.00x16
Optional tires: 4pr 8.55x15 m&s, $55; H78x15 m&s, $82; H78x15 wsw, $114.

Front axle capacity, lb 2000
Optional 3000
Front spring rating, lb (at pad) (4 cyl) 875, (V-6) 865
Optional 1240

Rear axle capacity 2500
Optional 3000
Rear spring rating, lb (at pad) 1240
Optional 1850 (V-6) $20

Additional suspension options: HD springs & shocks (4-cyl), $29; (V-6) $35. Dealer installed front air springs, $48; rear, $37.

ACCOMMODATION

Standard seat ......bucket (driver only)
Optional: passenger's bucket, $74; 1/3 passenger seat, $65; 2/3 driver seat, $24; rear bench, $88.
Head room, front/rear, in.: (fabric top) 39.5.
Pedal to seatback, max 35.5
Heater & defroster .... std
Tinted glass ....not available
Air conditioning ....not available
Load space with rear seat removed, cu ft 30

INSTRUMENTATION

Instruments: 90-mph speedometer, 99,999.9 odometer, fuel level, water temperature
Warning lights .... alternator, oil pressure
Optional ....none

DRIVE TRAIN

Transfer case .... Dana 18 2-spd
Transfer case ratio 2:46:1
Free-running front hubs ... dealer option
Limited slip differential $48

Rear axle type ......semi-floating hypoid
Final drive ratio 4.27:1
Optional final drive ratio 5.38:1

Standard transmission (with 4-cyl engine): Warner T90L 3-spd manual with non-synchro 1st gear.
Clutch dia., in. 9.25
Transmission ratios: 3rd 1.00:1
2nd 1.55:1
1st 3.34:1
Overdrive .... 0.75:1 (dealer option)

Standard transmission (with V-6): Warner T14A 3-spd manual, all synchro
Transmission ratios: 3rd 1.00:1
2nd 1.61:1
1st 3.10:1
Overdrive .... 0.75:1 (dealer option)

Optional transmission: Warner T98A heavy duty 4-spd manual with non-synchro 1st gear, $175.

Transmission ratios: 4th 1.00:1
3rd 1.69:1
2nd 3.09:1
1st 6.40:1
Overdrive .... 0.75:1 (dealer option)

GENERAL

Curb weight, lb (test model) 2550

Maximum laden weight 3750
With HD suspension 4750
Payload rating 1200
With HD suspension 2200

Wheelbase, in. 81.0
Track, front/rear 48.4/48.4
Overall length 135.6
Height 69.5
Width 61.8
Overhang, front/rear 22.5/32.0

Approach angle, degrees 45
Departure angle, degrees 30
Ramp breakover angle 30

Ground clearance: front differential .. 9.0
At rear differential 8.5
At oil pan 13.5
At transfer case (to shield) 9.5
At fuel tank (to shield) 12.5

Fuel tank capacity, U.S. gal 14.0

MAINTENANCE

Service intervals, normal use:
Oil change, mi 6000
Filter change 6000
Chassis lube 6000
Minor tuneup 6000
Major tuneup 12,000
Warranty, months/miles 12/12,000

OTHER OPTIONS

Cigar lighter $5.67
Draw bar $28
70-amp/hr battery $7.19
55-amp alternator $28
Tailgate tire mount .... not given

PERFORMANCE DATA	OFF PAVEMENT
Note: All performance data taken with maximum rated payload on board. Test model: V-6 engine, 3-spd transmission, full fabric top. List price, West Coast, $3625 (plus fabric top). **DRY PAVEMENT** Acceleration, time to speed, sec: 0-30 mph .... 3.1 0-45 mph .... 6.4 0-60 mph .... 11.2 0-70 mph .... 18.0 Maximum speed in gears: High range, 3rd (4000 rpm) .... 92 2nd (4500) .... 61 1st (4500) .... 32 Low range, 3rd (4500 rpm) .... 42 2nd (4500) .... 26 1st (4500) .... 13 Cruising speed at 3000 rpm .... 68 **BRAKE TESTS** Pedal pressure to achieve 1/2-g deceleration rate from 60 mph: 80. Fade: Percentage increase in pedal pressure for 6 successive stops from 60 mph: 27. Overall brake rating .... fair	Hillclimbing ability: Climb test hill no. 1 (47% grade) ..... yes Climb test hill no. 2 (56% grade) ..... yes Climb test hill no. 3 (63% grade) ..... yes Climb test hill no. 4 (69% grade) ..... yes Maneuverability .... excellent Turnaround capability .... excellent Comments: extremely maneuverable, excellent vision. **GENERAL** Heater rating .... poor Defroster effectiveness .... poor Wiper coverage .... adequate **FUEL CONSUMPTION** Normal driving, mpg .... 16 Off-pavement, test conditions, mpg . 8-10 Range, normal driving, mi .... 220 Range, off-pavement 110-140

The CJ-5 (CJ for Civilian Jeep) is called the Universal model and comes with an 81-in. wheelbase. There is also a long wheelbase CJ-6 Universal that is the same except it is built on a stretched chassis with a 121-in. wheelbase. The Universal is a narrow machine with a 48.4-in. track and is thus extremely well suited to getting into (and out of) those tight places.

The 134.2-cu-in. inline 4-cyl engine is standard and the ex-Buick lightweight V-6 with 160 horsepower is available for $211. With the V-6, an all-synchro 3-speed manual gearbox is standard. The heavy duty 4-speed manual (with non-sychro first gear) is also available as an option.

The Universal model comes in five body variations—pure open top, half tops of metal or fabric and full tops of metal or fabric. With the basic machine comes only the driver's seat but a passenger bucket, a 2/3rds-1/3rd split front seat and a rear bench seat are also available at extra cost. The instrumentation is simple and sparse, sitting right in the middle of the dashboard, and much of the military flavor is retained although there is a variety of colors available. The seating position is high and truck-like to give a commanding view of the road and the vision out over the short hood is nothing less than superb. With the Universal, you can see exactly where everything is and the driver is consequently far better able to judge what is going to scrape along the side.

There isn't a long list of options available for the Universal but the essentials are all there. You can get limited slip at the rear, for instance, there is a heavy duty suspension package available as an option and there's adequate room under the fenders to accept bigger tires than the 6.00 x 16s that come standard. Other popular options such as free-running front hubs and a tailgate-mounted spare are available as dealer options.

Driving Impressions

The CJ-5 is the off-pavement vehicle against which the performance of all other 4wd recreation vehicles is measured. Our test model, which had the V-6 Dauntless engine and all-synchro 3-speed gearbox, did everything we asked of it and did it so easily that we wondered if our test standards shouldn't have been more demanding. It climbed the hills like a goat, it slithered through our narrow canyon like a snake and it turned around almost as if it were on a turntable.

There's something friendly and comforting about a CJ-5. You take a big step up into it to get into the seat but once you're there, everything seems just right. The steering wheel is at the right angle and at just the right distance that you feel you're in full control. The gearbox, which is floor-mounted and has a conventional H-pattern shift, works just right and the V-6 engine gives it lots of peppy performance. The clutch and brake pedals are a bit heavier in operation than most passenger cars but these should not bother the normally strong of leg. The steering is reasonably quick yet not too sensitive and with the delightful view of the road out over the hood, you feel confident that you can put it exactly where you want it and not have to worry about expanses of sheet metal you can't see.

The ride is fairly stiff and, because of the short wheelbase, there's considerable fore-and-aft pitching over small ups and downs. With the V-6 there's plenty of performance to keep right up with any normal street and freeway traffic you're likely to encounter and the engine pulls strongly and with verve any time you depress the accelerator.

The creature comforts inside the fabric top with which our Universal was equipped are basic. There's a heater/defroster that rates as no better than fair with us and there's no ashtray that we could find. The fabric top flaps and rattles but seems reasonably draft free. The sidecurtains are flexible plastic and a zipper around the top half permits these to be opened for ventilation on not-too-cool days. The doors in this version are full-openers, giving plenty of room for ingress and egress. There's also a hang-on step below the door still to accommodate the short of leg.

Off the pavement, the CJ-5 with the V-6 is simply great, the most pure driving fun available in a 4wd recreation vehicle. You bounce around a bit, as you'd expect with the stiff springing, but this all seems part of the fun in the CJ-5. It isn't a luxury off-pavement cruiser, like the Wagoneer, so you don't apply the same standards. It goes where you want it to go, the straight-through transfer box lever gets you into whatever gear range you want without fuss, and that happy combination of quick steering, short wheelbase, the narrow body and excellent vision gives you a feeling of confidence like nothing else.

There's also a practical area behind the front seats for gear and while it is admittedly not very practical for more than two people, there is enough room that you could go on an extensive camping trip without having to give up all the amenities of civilization. The load-carrying capacity of the CJ-5 is more than adequate, in our opinion, as it has a rated payload of over 1000 lb–and it's difficult to see how you could get enough bulk aboard to upset its characteristic poise. The Universal model also has a drop-down tailgate, which adds 14 inches of bed length so it would be possible to construct a very practical cargo module even larger than the standard cargo area.

To sum up the CJ-5, we'd say it's the most fun to drive off the pavement, not all that bad on the hard road and, if you can live with its small size so far as passenger-carrying and bulk-carrying are concerned, you'll soon begin to regard it as a member of the family.

JEEP CJ-5

4WD OWNER SURVEY REPORT

THE JEEP CJ-5 Universal, descendent of the World War II military Jeep, represents over 30 years of development in the 4wd vehicle field. Being the original American 4-wheeler, the Jeep has served as the inspiration for a growing line of recreation vehicles from other manufacturers; yet, in spite of similarities, the Jeep has a character all its own. Or as one reader put it, "Jeeps are the real thing."

Today's Jeep, the CJ-5 Universal, is a somewhat refined version of the renowned military Jeep of the '40s. Powered by an inline, 4-cylinder, 114-brake horsepower engine, or by an optional V-6, 160-bhp powerplant (mostly the latter), the CJ-5 commands a $3023 base price, which pays for the small 6-cyl. engine, a 3-speed manual transmission, one seat (the driver's) 4-ply 6.00-16 tires and, of course, 4-wheel-drive. With a modest number of performance and convenience comfort items, the base price can easily exceed $3400.

In the 30 years since their inception, Jeeps have become firmly entrenched in the American motoring scene. It was no surprise then that we received 275 surveys from CJ-5 owners, plus a substantial number of surveys from military and CJ-2 owners. To achieve an accurate sampling of the CJ-5 scene we tabulated information derived from 1969, '70 and '71 model Universals. After excluding late-model Jeeps with less than 5000 miles on their odometers, we were left with 101 statistically acceptable surveys, which told us plenty about the CJ-5 and their owners.

The CJ-5 is almost everywhere. The largest concentration of Jeeps was found in the Southwest (California, Nevada, Arizona, New Mexico, and Texas), where 30% of our respondents reside–not a very surprising statistic when one considers that most uncluttered land is found in this part of the United States. Eighteen percent of our CJ-5 surveys came from the South, 16% from the Northeast, and 13% from the Midwest. Twelve percent of our replies came from the Rocky Mountain and Plains states, while 11% trickled in from the Northwest.

Though the V-6 aluminum engine is considered an option, 98% of our CJ-5 owners found it a "must" for their Jeep. Less than 2% of our sample CJ-5s were equipped with either the 4-cylinder stock powerplant or a V-8 conversion.

CJ-5 owners did not display the same enthusiasm for the optional 4-speed transmission as they did for the V-6 engine and a relatively small number of Jeeps, slightly less than 10%, were equipped with the 4-speed.

As far as other manufacturer/dealer options are concerned, CJ-5 owners responded in a pattern similar to that of owners of other 4wds. Ninety-six percent of our Jeep owners had ordered free-running front hubs, while 94% had chosen bucket seats. Sixty-nine percent of the owners had ordered limited slip differentials for their machines, and 61%, radios. Twenty-six percent opted for an overdrive, while 21% either ordered the factory-approved, dealer-installed Ramsey winch or hung some other winch on later.

Seventy-three percent of our CJ-5 respondents bought their vehicles new and 89% used their vehicles for daily transportation. Sixty-six percent of the owners expressed an interest in competition, with 67% acting as spectators, and 47% becoming involved in actual competition. Most popular events included races, rallies, and tours (in that order), with a small number of hillclimbs thrown in for good measure.

Less than half of our CJ-5 owners (46%) rated dealer service as "good." Twenty-five percent found service "fair," and 27% considered it "poor." Two percent called dealer service "very poor," indicating more than average displeasure with their local Jeep representatives. Twelve percent of the CJ-5 owners complained about the unavailability of spare parts, while 7% claimed that their dealers "did not know enough about 4wd." Seven percent reported that they do their own servicing. This puts Jeep dealers someplace about in the middle so far as owners' opinions of dealers go–better than Bronco dealers (35% rated "good"), but well below International dealers (64% "good").

CJ-5 owners equipped their vehicles with dozens of aftermarket accessories, more than any other make included in this series. Forty-five percent installed rollbars in their Jeeps, while 18% added oil, water, and temperature gauges. Fourteen percent equipped their 4wds with citizens band radios, and another 14% bolted on spare tire carriers. Tachometers were added by 13% of our respondents. Driving lights, steering stabilizers, accessory tops, and snow plows were installed by 5-10% of our owners.

Thirty-five percent of the CJ-5 owners have equipped their vehicles with larger-than-standard tires. Most popular tire among the replacements was the Gates XT Commando 10-15, followed quite closely by the 9.00-15 tire of the same make. Firestone's Super All Track 9.00-15, Inglewood's Stagger Block L70-15, Mitco's 9.55-15 and 9.00-15, and Thompson's Trailblazer 9.00-15 accounted for lesser percentages (3% or less per brand) of the total replacement tire picture.

A large percentage of CJ-5 owners (over 70%) used wider-than-stock wheels in conjunction with either their stock tires (8.55-15 or smaller) or with the aforementioned replacement tires. Eight-inch wide rims were the most popular choice among CJ-5 owners, with 10-inch rims the next choice.

From a mechanical standpoint the CJ-5 seemed afflicted by a surprising number of ills, some of them major. Three owners (two '69 models, one '71) claimed that they experienced engine breakage on their CJ-5s. In all cases the trouble was laid to improper assembly at the factory or to poor quality control, and one owner said that the crankshaft of his CJ-5 was "damaged during assembly." The factory honored the warranty in each instance; even in one case where the engine was replaced at 15,000 miles.

Problems which occurred in greater frequency (up to 20%) happily were of a less serious nature. Speedometer breakage or cable failure represented the lion's share of the CJ-5's instrument problems, reported by 20% of the owners. Cooling system difficulties (broken hoses and fittings) and clutch linkage failures accounted for 19 and 18% (respectively) of the Jeep's breakdowns. Starter malfunctions (15%) and transmission breakage (13%) contributed substantially to the CJ-5's mechanical shortcomings.

Troubles reported by 5-10% of the owners included U-joint failure, windshield wiper system breakage, differential problems and alternator malfunctions. In reference to the alternator, several CJ-5 owners reported that the Prestolite unit used on some Jeeps was "troublesome," and that they replaced the device with an Autolite alternator when a breakdown occurred. In all, mechanical problems were reported in every category from alternator to wiper motor, which may explain why one disgruntled owner charged, "Boy, I got a lemon when I bought this rig."

Several CJ-5 owners reported that

at times the front driveshaft hits the starter motor. One inventive enthusiast offered this solution: "Put longer shackles on the front springs."

Jeep owners liked a variety of things about their CJ-5s and we almost ran out of room on our tabulation forms trying to keep track of them all. In larger percentages, 35% of the owners said they liked the optional V-6 engine, while 29% liked the Jeep's compact size. Twenty-three percent lauded the CJ-5s maneuverability, and 9% praised its rugged construction. Eight percent of the owners liked the vehicle's light weight or weight distribution (they called the Jeep "well balanced"), while in identical percentages other owners praised its handling, its fuel economy, and its accessory line. Smaller percentages of owners liked the CJ-5's versatility and the see-all-around driving position. One small group, numbering 3%, liked the CJ-5 because "it's a Jeep."

The CJ-5's negative traits were revealed in the "Five Worst" segment of our survey. Though there were many individual complaints, there were few general gripes. The largest percentage of grumblings, 16%, centered around the Jeep's heater/defroster system which owners called "inadequate," especially in colder areas of the country. Nine percent of the owners complained about their vehicle's cramped interior, 8% about its rough ride, and another 8% about oil and water leaks. Six percent of the CJ-5 owners were unhappy about gear whine and engine noise, 5% disliked the vehicle's "sloppy" steering, and another 5% were dissatisfied with the Jeep's convertible top, which they said was "hard to raise."

Looking to the future, 70% of the owners reported that they would buy another 4wd vehicle. Of that number, 40% said they would buy another CJ-5. While the figures themselves are lower than those reported by owners of other makes of 4wds, the comments received in conjunction with these figures indicate that Jeep owners have a strong attachment to the marque, and that they enjoy the CJ-5 because (as one owner punned), "It's so universal." 4WD

SUMMARY: JEEP CJ-5

Most Popular Mfgr/Dealer Options

Free-running hubs
V-6 engine
Limited slip
Radio
Overdrive
Winch
Top

Most Popular Accessories Added by 10% or More of Owners

Rollbar or rollcages
Gauges
CB radio
Tachometer
Spare tire mount

Added by 5-10% of Owners

Tow bar
Snow plow
Driving lights
Steering stabilizer
Tape player

Troubles Reported by 5-10% of Owners

U-joints
Steering
Differential
Front springs
Rear springs
Transfer case
Alternator

Reported by 10-20% of Owners

Speedometer
Cooling system
Clutch
Starter
Transmission

Reported by Over 20% of Owners

None

Five Best Features

Performance (V-6)
Maneuverability
Size
Ruggedness
Fuel economy

Five Worst Features

Heater/defroster
Interior cramped
Rough ride
Oil/water leaks
Sloppy steering

Wheels/Tires

Owners using larger-than-standard tires 35%

How Owners Feel About Jeep Dealers

Rated "good" 46%
Rated "fair" 25%
Rated "poor" 29%

New or Used?

Bought new 73%
Bought used 27%

Buy Another?

Will buy another 4wd 70%
Will buy another CJ-5 . . . . 40%

JEEP ACCESSORIES

THE WORDS "four-wheel-drive" and Jeep are almost synonymous—quite understandable, since the Jeep was the first of the 4wd recreational vehicles. Not only that, the Jeep lineup includes a variety of 4wd vehicles from the CJ-5 on through the Commando and Wagoneer to the Jeep trucks. With such dedication to 4wd you'd expect American Motors Jeep to offer a more complete line of accessories for their machines. Such is not the case. Jeep's accessory inventory is sparse (Chevrolet's is much better), and includes most off-road equipment necessities, but few luxuries. So, Jeep people are forced to turn to the after-market folks for items such as auxiliary fuel tanks, heavy-duty bumpers, wide wheels and tow bars.

One of the people Jeep enthusiasts turn to, at least in Southern California, is Brian Chuchua, who calls himself "Mr. Jeep." A Jeep dealer as well as a Baja car builder and racer, he is well aware of the Jeep owner's needs and has designed a line of accessories that fills most of them.

Chuchua's wares includes a rubber-dipped rollbar for the Universal and CJ series ($69.95); Warn and Ramsey winches ($346-440) for all Jeep vehicles; gas tank and transfer case/transmission skid plates for Universals, CJs and Commandos ($8.40 to $23.35); wrap-around steel bumpers for most Jeep products (about $42); Kelly and Warn free-running front hubs for all Jeeps ($68); Kayline and Whitco convertible tops for the CJs ($120 to $175); Borg-Warner and Warn overdrives for the whole line ($179 and $218.78 respectively), plus dozens of little items that make off-road driving more pleasurable (or possible).

For the competition-minded 4wd enthusiast, Chuchua offers fiberglass body components which replace the steel body parts used on CJ and military series Jeeps. Brian claims that the 'glass components provide a 50% saving in weight over the factory steel units. He sells the fenders for $48.80 each, the hood for $55.84, and the body itself for $383.50. The 'glass parts are not for everyone, but certainly worth consideration by racers.

One useful little accessory for CJs is the Chuchua tailgate extension, a storage box that bolts onto the rear of the Universal, behind the tailgate. Constructed of fiberglass, the lightweight compartment provides extra storage space for cross-country touring (on and off the road) and is priced at $49.95.

It would take a 50-page catalog to list all of the accessories Chuchua sells for Jeep 4wd recreational vehicles. Brian has just such a catalog and it's priced at $1, available from Brian Chuchua's Four Wheel Drive Center, P.O. Box 301, Fullerton, CA 92632.

JEEP

PERFORMANCE AND COMFORT ITEMS FOR JEEP vehicles include this partial listing of accessories:

1—Ramsey power winch for CJ-5, $375.

2—Rollbar for CJ-5, $46.95 (standard), $69.95 (foam dipped).

3—Auxiliary fuel tank for CJ-5, $37.95.

4—Carpet kit for CJ-5, $40.95.

5—Side tire mount for CJ-5, $7.20.

6—Kelly free-running front hubs, $68 per pair.

7—Warn free-running front hubs, $68 per pair.

8—Tow bar, $39.50 (painted), $75 (chromed).

9—Adapter kit (4-speed to Jeep transfer case), $185.

10—Skid plate for CJ-5 transmission and transfer case, $8.40.

11—Wide wheel (steel, 15-8), $22.95.

12—Tierod, one piece, CJ-5, $8.95.

13—Heco steering stabilizer kit, $26.40.

Jeep, Wagoneer, Commando (Jeepster), and Jeep truck accessories not shown include King, Belleview, and Rhino winches, skid plates, tire mount kits, wide wheels, overdrive, canvas and steel tops (for Universals and CJ-5s), and jerry can carriers, plus other miscellaneous items. A catalog listing all Jeep 4wd accessories is available for $1 from Brian Chuchua's Four Wheel Drive Center, P.O. Box 301, Fullerton, CA 92632.

Since the early days of automation when the invention of the internal combustion engine directed the world into an age of motion, there have been milestones, both in development, in engineering and in memorable models—usually a vehicle which was cheap to build, mass-produced and had certain appeal to the buying public. The first of these cars was undeniably the Ford Model T and half a century later the Mini must share the same fame. Between these two models came the war, a period of technical advancement unhoped for in peacetime. Seemingly unsurmountable problems disappeared under a storm of thought, while some surprisingly simple, imaginative, and highly worthwhile ideas emerged. One of these was the Jeep.

Prior to the start of hostilities a utility vehicle of quarter ton capacity had been put out to tender by the US Army to three manufacurers—Willys-Overland, the American Bantam Co and Ford. (Ford always feature somewhere don't they ?) Each put forward their own proposals, and although model production started for each of the three types, a standard mark, the MA appeared, soon to be replaced by the MB model widely recognised as the Jeep.

The Jeep had a ' flathead ' engine of 2198cc, a three-speed gearbox with synchromesh on second and third gears a two-speed transfer box, and of course four wheel drive. A doorless functional body with fold-flat windscreen, cutaway front wings and slatted rad grille all added up to a no-frills form of transport. Its ageless design was produced until 1970 in France by the firm of Hotchkiss for the French army. Though many countries' armed forces have used the Jeep, and replaced it with more sophisticated hardware, it is by no means indicative that the replacement machinery is superior.

I think it is safe to say that if you buy a Jeep you are an enthusiast as it is a fairly rare beast in this island of ours, most MBs going to France in '44 and '45 and nearly all subsequent army surplus being exported or junked.

If you really feel you must have a Jeep the best place to look is in the columns of the Exchange and Mart, where very likely you'll find a runner as well as some which have fallen into disuse. Another idea, and here a quick plug, join the All Wheel Drive Club who are a good crowd and always ready with advice.

Certainly the pleasure of owning a Jeep must be the imagination you have to exercise to keep it rolling. Most parts are available and amazingly many modern car parts can, er, be adapted so be friendly to all the storemen as you may want to root about in their stores bins one fine day. Condition is going to vary from good all the way down to quite horrific. Bodywise, floors and fuel tank wells are water traps and when bailed dry they rust. Body corners rust out and depending on the way the Jeep has been left standing, used or stored in fact almost anything could have happened. First consideration then, if you're not a panel beater or handy with tinsnips and a torch, is to get some quotes for panel repairs. Out of all replacement parts the body is the most difficult.

The mechanical wear will be relative to usage and could well be considerable. If it's been standing for some time the motor may be seized with a simple case of a gummed ring or a sticking valve. On the other hand if water's found its way in, the position could be much worse. However I know of engines which are running quite successfully with rust-pitted bores. Pistons, valves, shells, rings and gaskets are all available, and expense to do a full rebuild should be in the £50 region providing no major components have to be replaced and including machine shop services.

In the gearbox the synchro wears out and if the gears are worn badly they'll jump out under load. As with most four wheel drive transfer cases, the large output gear seems to cause a good rumble when it's tired. Universal joints need replacing and are still available. Axles and diffs are strong but mind the half shafts, they break if abused.

You like rewiring? It might well be a must and would save you the aggravation of electrical failure. Electrics on a Jeep are important as it's only a six volt system, and big sparks are really useful. Dynamos and starters can still be bought from a few specialists, but my goodness are they expensive! They're very heavy duty and are usually repairable in an electrical workshop. It's possible to simplify the loom on a Jeep to just plain lights, brakes, and ignition circuits, as if they had radio filtration equipment fitted you can get in a real tangle.

The main proportion of Jeeps seen in this country are the MB wartime models. Its successor, the M38, very similar in appearance and mechanics, had twenty-four volt electrics system and a few body refinements. It's hard to tell the difference. The M38 was built between 1950 and '52. The other Jeeps that may be seen is the M38A1, a much rounder vehicle, with an F-head engine and 24 volt electrics—not too many of those about either.

Tyres are the same size as Land-Rover and the rear of our Offroad Runner, sixteen inchers (wonder when I'll get a drive in that!). If you want the original military-style tread, some research into the products of the lesser known tyre makers will be rewarding.

Cross-country performance is phenomenal—won't quite climb the side of a house but . . . The MB is much lighter than a Land Rover or a Champ, has lightness, power and long axle travel and a short wheelbase. All goes to make a great little slugger when the going gets tough.

Now the prices, all very approximate I'm afraid; say £100 to £300 for an MB runner in various stages of repair, prices for the M38 and M38A1 all appear to be over three hundred at the moment. **RP**

JEEP CJ-5 V-8

WHEN THE TALK gets around to the longevity of a particular model of car, someone invariably brings up the Volkswagen Beetle. But compared to the Jeep, the Beetle really isn't in the show. The Jeep has evolved during the more than 30 (yes, 30) years since the first model came off the production line, yet in spite of all its changes, that vehicle is still *the* basic 4-wheel-drive recreation vehicle around which all other 4wds evolved. We're among those who hope that the Jeep continues forever. The world of off-pavement motoring wouldn't be the same without it.

4 WD TEST

The 1972 CJ-5 (forget that it was previously called the "Universal," it isn't anymore) is the latest version of the basic machine, and in spite of several differences between it and its predecessors, the Jeep still retains all its basic character as the sprightly granddaddy who can still show these upstarts in the 4wd field a thing or two.

The 1972 CJ-5 (CJ stands for "Civilian Jeep," in case you've wondered) is notable for several reasons. It gets a new assortment of engines, it's slightly bigger, it has better brakes, different steering and an assortment of other variations.

The engine line is all new to the 1972 CJ-5. The venerable F-head 134-cu. in. inline 4, which has been standard since we can't remember when, is no longer available in this country, though it will continue to be built for export. The ex-Buick V-6, which was the optional engine in the past few years, has gone out of production. Now there are three American Motors engines—a 232-cu. in. inline 6 which is standard equipment, and a 258-cu. in. inline 6 and a 304 V-8 which are optional. The 20-in.-longer CJ-5 and the 1972 Commando share the same engine alignment, running gear and suspension.

The transmission selection for the CJ-5 has also changed. No more is the old manual 3-speed with non-synchro-first the standard gearbox. Now there's a fully-synchronized, floor-shifter 3-speed as standard, with a heavy-duty manual

(non-synchro first) 4-speed available with the two 6-cylinder engines. If you want the 304 V-8 engine, you have to accept the standard 3-speed transmission. No, the CJ-5 isn't available with the 3-speed automatic as is the Commando.

In overall size, the CJ-5 has gotten slightly bigger again. The wheelbase is now 84.0 inches (was 81.0) in order to accommodate the longer engines that are now being used. The overall length has increased a bit as well, and is now 138.9 (instead of 135.6). The width and height stay the same as before.

There are also other changes in the running gear. At the front there is a new axle, the Dana 30, which replaces the Dana 27 of sainted memory. This increases the track marginally to 51.5 inches (from 48.4), but the greatest benefit is that this new axle with its open-end balljoint mechanism has a greater turning angle and reduces the turning circle to just 32.0 ft (from 38.6). The front springs have been increased in capacity to handle the weight of the heavier engines, but there is no change in payload rating. The steering mechanism is also different. A new recirculating ball system replaces the old cam-and-lever arrangement, and there are fewer steering joints, making servicing easier and reducing the tendency toward sloppiness as the parts wear. With the new steering system, the overall steering ratio is slower, which reduces the effort but increases the amount of wheel-turning that is required. Optional power steering is available with all engines.

At the rear the CJ-5 sports a new axle, this one with a track of 50.0 inches (instead of 48.4) and a capacity of 3000 lb. (previously 2500).

Other changes in the power train include the use of the Dana 20 transfer case which uses a low range ratio of 2.03, rather than the tighter 2.46:1 of earlier models. High range is still 1.00:1. The transfer case also has a longer stalk for easier shifting. With the new engine line-up, a 3.73:1 final drive ratio is standard with all engines, but there is a shorter 4.27:1 ratio available on special order.

The brakes are larger than before and now 11x2-inch drums are used in place of the 10x2s. Power brakes are an option with the 304 V-8 engine. The brake and clutch pedals are suspended from the cowl and no longer come up through the floorboards. Anyone who has ever experienced a jet of water up the pant leg in an older Jeep will welcome the new pedals. The new clutch is also larger (10.5 vs. 9.25 inches), the parking brake is now foot- and not hand-operated and the fuel tank holds 16.5, not 14 gallons.

There's still a practical assortment of heavy-duty equipment available, including a heavy-duty frame, fuel tank skid plate, extra cooling capacity radiator, plus heavy-duty shocks and springs.

Another interesting option that is new to the list is a fixed tailgate, used in place of the standard drop-down version. The fixed tailgate allows the spare tire to be mounted on the rear instead of on the side of the vehicle. The side-mounted spare has always been something of an annoyance when the Jeep is in really close quarters.

There are no optional trim packages with the CJ-5 and the seating is the same as before, with the driver bucket seat standard and the passenger's seat optional. A 2/3-1/3 split front bench and a rear bench seat are available as options. These are new seats, by the way, full-foam and firmly padded.

In the luxury option class, you may be glad to know that you can now have an ashtray in your CJ-5 (no more rubbing out butts on the floorboards). There is a pair of optional gauges for the oil pressure and ammeter. These gauges are located on the left side of the dashboard. The single unit speedo/odo/water/fuel gauge/warning light cluster is still located in the middle of the dash where it has always been. Why? Because that location allows both lefthand and righthand drive models to be built without having to make two different dashboards. Some of the old military practicality still shows.

DRIVING IMPRESSIONS

Our 1972 CJ-5 came equipped with the top of the line options. There was the 304 V-8 with the sole transmission choice, the 3-speed manual gearbox, plus power steering and power brakes. There was also a nice, solid, reassuring rollbar and the optional Whitco vinyl-coated full-fabric top. The West Coast price of our test CJ-5 as equipped was $3858.

If it wasn't a CJ-5, we'd probably find dozens of things to complain about. It's hard to get into, and even harder to get out of. Vision is restricted with the top on, the steering isn't quick, and the gearbox is short of stalk. The spare tire hangs out on the side, cargo room is sparse, and the highway ride is

JEEP CJ-5 V-8

PRICE

Basic list, FOB Toledo, Ohio ... $3023

Standard equipment: 232 inline 6 engine, 3-speed manual transmission, 4wd, driver's seat only, heater/defroster.

Other prices for options are included in data below.

ENGINES

Standard engine .... 232 inline 6
Bore x stroke, in. 3.75x3.50
Displacement, cu. in. 232
Compression ratio 8.0:1
Net horsepower @ rpm ... 100 @ 3600
Net torque @ rpm, lb.-ft. .. 185 @ 1800
Type fuel required .... regular

Optional 258 inline 6 .... $56
Bore x stroke, in. 3.75x3.90
Compression ratio 8.0:1
Net horsepower @ rpm ... 110 @ 3500
Net torque @ rpm, lb.-ft. .. 195 @ 2000
Type fuel required .... regular

Optional 304 V-8 .... $130
Bore x stroke, in. .... 3.75 x 3.44
Compression ratio 8.3:1
Net horsepower @ rpm ... 150 @ 4200
Net torque @ rpm, lb.-ft. .. 245 @ 2500
Type fuel required .... regular

DRIVE TRAIN

Transfer case .... Dana 20 2-speed
Transfer case ratios ... 2.03 & 1.00:1
Free-running front hubs $98
Limited slip differential (R) $61

Rear axle type ... semi-floating hypoid
Final drive ratio 3.73:1
Optional final drive ratio 4.27:1

Standard transmission .. 3-spd. manual
Clutch dia., in. 10.5
Transmission ratios:

	6-cyl.	V-8
3rd	1.00:1	1.00:1
2nd	1.61:1	1.83:1
1st	3.10:1	3.00:1

Optional transmission: heavy-duty 4-speed manual (non-synchro first); not available with V-8 engine, $175
Transmission ratios:
4th 1.00:1
3rd 1.69:1
2nd 3.09:1
1st 6.32:1

CHASSIS & BODY

Body/frame: steel ladder frame with separate steel body.

Brakes: 11x2-in. drums, front & rear.
Brake swept area, sq. in. 276
Power brakes (with V-8 only) $46

Steering type, std. ... recirculating ball
Steering ratio 24:1
Turns, lock-to-lock 6.0
Power steering $148
Power steering ratio 17.5:1
Turning circle, ft. 32.9

Wheel size, std. .... 15-6 K
Optional wheel sizes ...... 16-4.5 E
Tire size, std: 7.35-15 4PR
Optional tire sizes: up to H78-15 or 6.00-16

Front axle capacity, lb. 2300
Optional .... none
Front spring rating at pad, lb. 855
Optional 1300
Rear axle capacity, lb. 300
Optional .... none
Rear spring rating at pad, lb. 1240
Optional 1260

ACCOMMODATION

Standard seats .... driver's bucket
Optional: passenger bucket ($74), 2/3-1/3 split front bench ($89), rear bench ($92).
Headroom, in. (cloth top) 41.0
Pedal-to-seatback, max. 33.0
Seat-to-ground 36.5
Heater & defroster .... std.
Tinted glass .... not available
Air conditioning .... not available
Load space (w/o rear seat), in. 36x32x43

INSTRUMENTATION

Instruments: 90-mph speedo, 99,999.9 odo, fuel level, engine temperature.
Warning lights: oil pressure, alternator
Optional: oil pressure & ammeter, $17

MAINTENANCE

Service intervals, normal use, miles:
Oil change 6000
Filter change 6000
Chassis lube 6000
Minor tuneup 6000
Major tuneup 12,000
Warranty, months/miles ... 12/12,000

GENERAL

Curb weight, lb. (test model) 2935

Maximum laden weight, lb. 3750
With HD suspension 4500

Wheelbase, in. 84.0
Track, front/rear 51.5/50.0
Overall length 138.9
Height 69.5
Width 61.8
Overhang, front/rear 22.6/32.0

Approach angle, degrees 45
Departure angle 28
Ramp breakover angle 30

Ground clearances, inches:
Front differential 8.75
Rear differential 8.5
Oil pan 14.5
Transfer case 14.5
Fuel tank 12.8

Fuel tank capacity, U.S. gal. 16.5
Auxiliary tank .... none

OTHER OPTIONS

55-amp. alternator $28
70-amp. battery $12
Cigar lighter $7
Draw bar $28
Heavy-duty frame $20
Padded instrument panel $38
Fuel tank skid plate $20
Spare tire tailgate mount $10
Sun visors $14

PERFORMANCE DATA

Test model: 304 V-8 engine, 8.55-15B Goodyear Suburbanite tires, bucket seats, optional gauges, power steering, power brakes, cloth top, rollbar, free-running front hubs, limited slip (rear), heavy-duty suspension, 4.27:1 final drive ratio, etc. West Coast list price, $3858 (does not include rollbar or fabric top).

DRY PAVEMENT	
Acceleration, time to speed, sec.:	
0-30 mph	3.7
0-45 mph	7.0
0-60 mph	13.0
0-70 mph	19.0
Maximum speed in gears (4.27:1 final drive):	
High range, 3rd (4200 rpm)	82
2nd (4200 rpm)	45
1st (4200 rpm)	28
Low range, 3rd (4200 rpm)	40
2nd (4200 rpm)	22
1st (4200 rpm)	14
Cruising speed at 3000 rpm	58.5

BRAKE TESTS

Pedal pressure to achieve 1/2-g deceleration rate from 60 mph, 45
Fade: Percentage increase in pedal pressure for 6 stops from 60 mph, 35%

Overall brake rating	good

OFF PAVEMENT	
Hillclimbing ability:	
Climb hill no. 1 (47% grade)	yes
Climb hill no. 2 (56% grade)	yes
Climb hill no. 3 (63% grade)	yes
Climb hill no. 4 (69% grade)	yes
Maneuverability	excellent
Turnaround capability	excellent

Comments: Still the standard to which all 4wds must be compared.

GENERAL	
Heater rating	poor
Defroster effectiveness	poor
Wiper coverage	adequate

FUEL CONSUMPTION	
Normal driving, mpg	15
Off-pavement, test conditions	9-10
Range, normal driving, mi.	250
Range, off-pavement	150-165

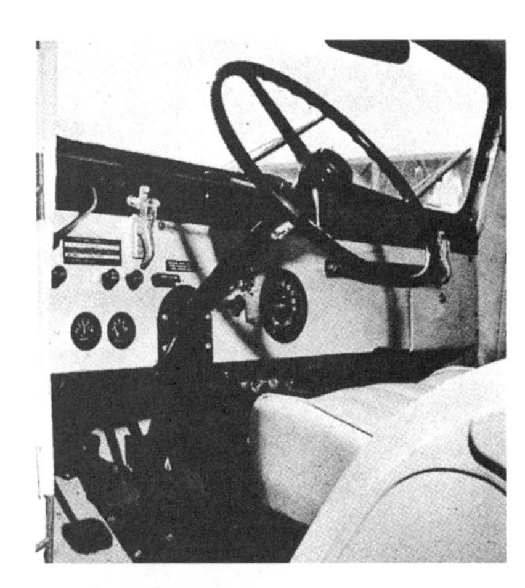

hard. The cloth top flaps and rumbles and the horn sounds ridiculous.

But forget all that. When you buy a CJ-5, this is what you get and you might as well accept the vehicle for what it is. Enjoy it for what it can do and admit from the start that the CJ-5 is the real thing. This is the machine that paved the way for the whole 4wd recreation vehicle thing and you honestly owe it to yourself to make its acquaintance. We enjoyed every minute of our time in the CJ-5, especially when we scooted off from a stoplight in a dragstrip start to amaze and mystify the unsuspecting. And we also enjoyed letting the Jeep have its head off the pavement where it really demonstrates its class.

We had wondered what the effect of the 304 V-8 was going to be. We admit that we're not altogether power-mad and we thought the old V-6 had just about the right amount of poke for the CJ-5. The V-6 would highway cruise without complaint and possessed a good amount of usable torque. After driving the V-8, we have to confess that we thought the bigger engine added to the overall fun. Of course, it comes close to using up all the handling capability of the suspension, but it sure keeps you awake and on your toes. The gears are short so the all-out top speed potential is only mildly fast (just over 80 mph) but the big V-8 pulls without hesitation right up until you begin to worry about engine speed.

Going up through the gears you quickly discover that there's a lot of engine and fan noise coming through the firewall. Once you figure out that it is just noise and that the engine still wants to keep pulling, you relax and enjoy it. The feeling of exhilarating performance is largely imaginary because the short wheelbase, the high-up seating position and the rush of the wind all combine to give you the unmistakable illusion of speed.

The new brakes on the CJ-5, plus the power assist, give the vehicle stopping power like no CJ-5 has ever known. These brakes aren't overboosted (45 lb. pressure for a half-g stop), which just might stand you on your nose with this machine. There was a moderate amount of fade (35%) in our "six stops from 60" fade test, but not enough to be bothersome. We counted the previous brakes of the CJ-5 as "fair" but these are much better–efficient enough to be worth a "good" rating.

The new steering system of the CJ-5 seems to us to be a trade-off between slower steering and longer life. At parking speed on hard pavement the slower ratio does reduce the steering effort. In addition, the down-the-road behavior isn't so twitchy as before and maybe this isn't all bad, considering the power of the V-8 engine. Off the pavement, however, the steering is dead easy and there it takes more wheel winding to make a quick turn. And, if it's any concession, you can turn more sharply, thanks to the new front axle. So, as we said, you give a little and you take a little with the CJ-5.

As always, rough-country driving brings out the Jeep's true nature. The CJ-5 is nimble and quick and, at a mere suggestion, will jump over objects much larger than a candlestick. The big V-8 engine gives the '72 CJ-5 off-pavement speed like no CJ-5 has ever had before and waltzing up steep inclines has never been so easy. It also has sufficient power to get the inattentive into more trouble more quickly, in case that's a consideration. For everyday practicality, we think the medium-size 6-cylinder engine might fill most drivers' needs quite well.

The CJ-5 V-8 can do as much or more than any other 4wd recreation vehicle in the world. In other words, it still remains the standard by which the performance of all such machines must be measured. It's still the "Real Jeep."

Road Testing the newest version of the classic CJ-5

RIP ROARIN' RENEGADE

By Bill Sanders

When you road test the CJ-5, you should do it with aplomb and a certain amount of distinction. After all, the CJ-5 is sort of the epitome of four wheeling. Other manufacturers build highly competent 4x4 rigs and many of them can perform equally with the Jeep. But, deep down in the pit of the stomach, every four wheeler, whether he'll admit it or not, knows that the CJ-5 is really nitty gritty when it comes to four wheeling.

To bring as much distinction to a CJ-5 road test as possible, FOUR WHEELER decided to test the all new CJ-5 with V8 power *and* in *Renegade* trim. The Renegade, in case you didn't know, is the dress-up, customized version of the CJ-5, if such a thing is possible. It's a limited edition model, and, according to Jeff Wright, Jeep sales manager, "The Renegade was developed for the Jeep enthusiast who likes a lot of custom touches as well as all the power options that are available."

The basic Renegade dress-up package includes: American Racing, cast aluminum wheels with H78x15 white wall snow tires, a roll bar, dual outside mirrors, fender extenders (for wider tires), striped seat trim, a Renegade hood stripe and a choice of three wild Renegade paint colors, Yellow, Orange or Plum. That package costs $299.00. But, since all Renegade models are built identically, there are other extra cost options that you *must* take as part of the package. These include: A Trac-lok rear axle, 304 cu. in. V8 with two barrel carburetor, dual sun visors, heavy duty cooling, a rear seat, a fuel tank skid plate, a passenger side safety rail (to hang onto when the going gets rough), ammeter and oil-pressure gauges, and a solid back panel with a rear mounted spare tire. Even though you have to pay extra for these last mentioned options and you are required to take them as part of the package, they are all worth the money because they offer either safety or utility factors you wouldn't get in a straight, bare-bones CJ-5. Power brakes and power steering are also both optional items, and that *means* optional.

POWERTRAIN AND PERFORMANCE

The 304 V8 has a listed horsepower rating of 150 at 4,200 RPM. This compares to 100 hp for the standard 232 cu. in. six or 110 hp for the step up 258 cu. in. six. That big jump of 40 or 50 ponies really makes a difference for those of you used to pushing a Jeep with a six or a four banger. Of course, it's not a small

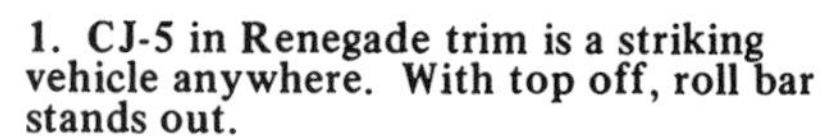

1. CJ-5 in Renegade trim is a striking vehicle anywhere. With top off, roll bar stands out.

2. With Whitco top in place, Renegade is ready for any weather.

3. Optional Amp and Oil pressure gauges are on lower left-hand side of instrument panel. Note brake release handle just above and left of steering column.

4. Hood stripe and name are distinctive.

5. 304 V8 engine fits well back against firewall. Engine compartment isn't too cluttered. Note power steering reservoir in front of left rocker-arm cover.

6. CJ-5 has new transfer case for '72. Operation is simple and easy.

7. American Racing cast aluminum wheels really dress up Renegade. Test rig had locking front hubs.

8. Glove box is small as usual. Note passenger safety rail (sissy bar) which is mandatory option with Renegade.

9. Ramsey winch and large front bumper extend far out in front.

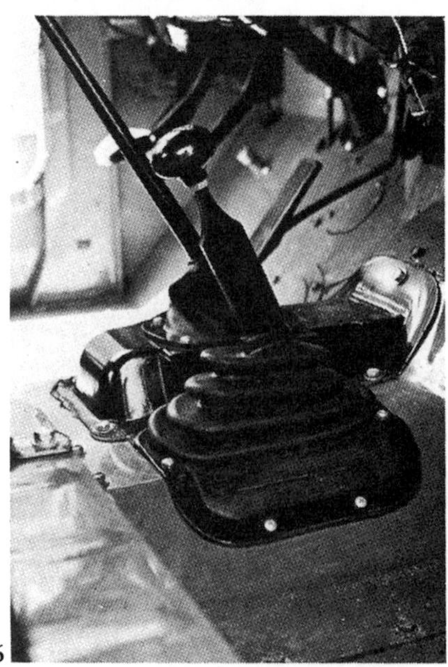

7

8

9

block Chevy, but the 304 is a lightweight block and it only costs $125.65 extra as a factory installation, compared to the higher cost of a conversion. Plus you have a warranty and the whole shot.

In a word, the 304 is a spunky little mill to have sitting under the hood and it is capable of really getting the CJ-5 off the dime. Our test vehicle had a front and rear axle ratio of 3.73:1, which may seem a pretty tall gear for off-road use. But the 3.73 seemed ideal in the test machine as it cruised at 70 mph easily on the highway with no excessive noise or engine strain. A 4.27:1 is also available for low gear lovers. Off-road, we had no problem climbing the steepest hills we could find. The 304 torque rating is 245 lbs.-ft. at 2,500 RPM. While this isn't the greatest torque in the world, it seems to get the job done. We don't think you'd want to go to any lower gears, unless you were planning on doing a little sand racing or something of that nature.

A three speed, floor mounted tranny is standard with every CJ-5 and is also standard with the Renegade, so you don't have to pay extra for that as an option. The three speed operates well in virtually every situation. Second gear is especially great on road, as it gives the little bob tail plenty of pickup. With the 304 and the three speed, acceleration from a standing start is quite brisk and can put a lot of surprised looks on people's faces getting away from stop lights. The transfer case and shifter are standard CJ-5 and we had no difficulty getting in or out of 4WD. Our test vehicle had locking front hubs, and thus the accompanying benefits that accrue to a vehicle when you have those little goodies as part of your front end package.

HANDLING, STEERING AND STOPPING

As mentioned above, power steering and brakes are both optional with the Renegade. This test machine had power steering, but manual brakes. The power steering certainly made turning and handling much easier with lots less effort. But we feel that one of those options compliments the other; if you order one, order both. Or, conversely, if you leave one off, leave both off. We picked this power steering/power brakes philosophy up from Zora Arkus-Duntov, the mastermind behind the Chevy Corvette. He set up Corvette option ordering in such a manner that if you order power steering you have to take power brakes and vice versa. We think this policy can apply to off-road vehicles as well. We noticed with the Renegade, power steering sort of lulled us into a certain psychological confidence. Then when hard braking was necessary, the manual brakes came as sort of a rude awakening. We weren't prepared for the heavy physical effort of braking, as that effort had been lacking with the steering. Anyway, it is something to think about when ordering any 4x4 vehicle. Our test Renegade also had, as an option, a Ramsey winch hanging away

out over the front end. With manual steering, the Renegade would have been a bear to turn, especially off-road in some of the places we took it in the mountains and desert. Incidentally, the winch was placed so far in front because the steering box on the Jeep extends so far in front itself.

Like any CJ-5, ours had a high roll center and getting around corners and through curves too fast caused a queazy feeling for a few minutes. That could be one of the initial hang-ups of the V8. With the power available, you find yourself going around corners on road a little over your head at first. You have to adjust to the vehicle.

The CJ-5 has a slightly wider front and rear tread in '72. That is a result of accommodating the new V8. There is a noticeable difference in lateral stability because of wider tread. The front has been widened by three inches to 51.5 in., and the rear is 50 in. wide, 1.5 in. wider than in previous models.

Also in the better handling department comes the Dana 30, open-end front axle. It replaces the old Dana 27 and minimizes the tendency to wheel

CJ-5 OPTIONS AND PRICES	
Base price	$2,955.00
Trac-Lok rear axle, 3.73 ratio	59.40
304 cu. in. V8 engine	125.65
Lighter and ash tray	8.65
Dual sun visors	13.55
Front passenger seat	72.10
Spare wheel lock	4.05
Heavy duty cooling	25.60
Rear seat, bucket style	89.35
Fuel tank skid plate	19.30
Power steering	143.25
Passenger seat safety rail	6.85
Padded instrument panel	31.90
Amp and oil gauges	16.65
Solid back panel with rear mounted spare	9.60
"Renegade" package	299.00
Includes: H78x15 whitewall Polyglas tires; cast wheels; roll bar; passenger side mirror; fender extenders; special seat trim; Renegade hood stripe; and Renegade special paint.	

CJ-5 SPECIFICATIONS	
Engine	304 cu. in. OHV V8
Horsepower	150 @ 4,200 RPM
Torque	245 lbs.-ft. @ 2,500 RPM
Carburetion	One 2-BBL.
Wheelbase	84 in.
Overall Length	142.1 in.
Overall Width	59.9 in.
Overall Height	69.5 in.
Front Overhang	22.6 in.
Rear Overhang	32.0 in.
Front Tread	51.5 in.
Rear Tread	50.0 in.
Minimum Ground Clearance	8.0 in.
Minimum Turning Circle	32.9 ft.
Front Leg Room	41.0 in.
Front Hip Room	55.4 in.
Curb Weight	2,437 lbs.
Gross Vehicle Weight (Standard)	3,750 lbs.
Gross Vehicle Weight (Maximum)	4,500 lbs.

CJ-5 GAS MILEAGE	On Road	Off Road
	11.4 to 12.2 mpg	8.9 to 10.0 mpg

10

10. **Fuel tank skid plate is also mandatory option, but is excellent item to have in rough stuff.**

shimmy, improves serviceability and maneuverability, and significantly improves the turning circle. The latter is one thing you'll notice as a big improvement over previous CJ's.

Except for the psychological effect on braking mentioned above, getting the CJ-5 stopped isn't too much of a problem. In panic brake tests there was a little pulling, but no appreciable fade. For '72, a foot operated parking brake replaces the old hand lever type. The parking brake release is now located on the dash to the left of the steering column. Also, for quieter operation, a new Dana 20 transfer case without parking brake replaces the old Dana 18 that had a park brake.

COMFORT, CONVENIENCE AND UTILITY

There are a variety of seating arrangements you can get with the ordinary CJ-5, single front bucket, an optional passenger front bucket, a 2/3-1/3 split front bench seat, and a rear bench. With the Renegade, you get a front bucket for the driver, the Bostrom full-foam style. Plus, you have to take a rear, bucket-style seat. A front passenger bucket is an option for $13.55, and we're sure most will opt for that.

The Renegade bucket seats are upholstered in a special black vinyl that looks like it should wear well and long, even with rough use. Seating is comfortable in the Renegade buckets, even if the usual bouncing CJ-5 ride hasn't changed much. The Renegade also has a padded dash that is also an option you have to take. It costs $31.90.

For convenience, ammeter and oil gauges are added at extra cost as part of the Renegade package. These are located on the lower edge of the dash, left of the steering column. The fuel and temperature gauges are in the usual location in the speedometer/odometer pod in the center of the dash. The ammeter and oil pressure gauges are in a spot that is a little difficult to look at without moving your head to the left. Our test vehicle had the new, optional lighter and ash tray, which is something pretty racy for rugged old Jeep! If you are a smoker, they do come in handy though. The new, solid back panel and rear mounted spare should help you get through narrower spots, plus the vehicle looks a little more sanitary with that set up. Our test machine came equipped with a spare wheel/tire lock that costs

Continued on page 74

Everything's Out Front

New styling, new steering, new power, new seats, new gearboxes, new axles, new U-joints, the old Jeep isn't anymore/By Chuck Koch

Being first is at once a curse and a blessing. Blessed because you started it all but cursed since you must suffer through comparisons to your offspring. So it is with the Jeep; a vehicle conceived by the long defunct American Bantam Car Company for the Army as a means to transport troops through practically impassable terrain which happily later turned out to be a form of relaxation and recreation for civilians. Because of its success in this task, the Jeep has been copied in part or in total by almost every major automobile manufacturer while Jeep relaxed in first place. Given enough time, bigger engineering departments and more money, these larger companies were able to make a 4WD vehicle that surpassed the Jeep in performance, coldly pushing it from the forefront of the market. Somewhere along in here, American Motors decided to get in the recreational vehicles biz and purchased Jeep. This arrangement first brought status quo, until everybody got happy in the new situation, but now AMC and Jeep have gotten their act together and produced the most improved Jeep to come along in years.

For 1972 the CJ-5 (meaning "civilian jeep" just as the name "Jeep" is a derivative of the initials from the official military name "General Purpose Vehicle") is upgraded in almost every major area. There is an entirely new engine line, a new transfer case, better brakes, different steering with a new front axle, overall dimensions are slightly bigger, and various other improvements that serve to make the new Jeeps that much more pleasurable to drive.

This year the three engines that power the new Jeeps are all American Motors Products; the venerable Dauntless V6 motor is now out of production while the old F-head in-line 4 cylinder engine is available only for export. Standard engine is the AMC 232 c.i. in-line OHV 6 that has a bore/stroke of 3.75 x 3.5 inches, and delivers 100 net hp at 3600 rpm and 185 lbs.-ft. of torque at 1800 rpm while an 8:1 compression ratio makes it possible to get 14 mpg of low-lead gasoline. Optional on the new CJ-5s are a 258 c.i. in-line 6 and a 304 c.i. OHV V8. The larger six is built from the same block as its smaller brother with a longer stroke (3.75 x 3.9-inch bore/stroke) accounting for the increased displacement. The engine produces 110 hp at 3500 rpm and 195 lbs.-ft. of torque at 2000 rpm. Fuel economy, though, falls off to a road test best of 11.6 mpg of low-lead gas. If Jeep really wanted to become competitive with its more performance-minded offspring, a V8 engine was essential and the 304-2v American Motors engine fills the bill. Its bore/stroke is 3.75 x 3.44 inches and the power is there for sure; 150 hp at 4200 rpm and 245 lbs.-ft. of torque at 2500 rpm. Although the 8.4:1 compression ratio theoretically makes it possible to run on low-lead gas, we found our best power and economy results came with leaded fuel.

Tied to these more powerful engines is a new standard floor-mounted all-synchronized 3-speed manual transmission. The shift throws are fairly short for an off-road machine and a larger clutch (10.5-inch diameter against the older 9.25 inches) makes engagement positive although pedal action is a bit too stiff. Also available, only in the 6 cylinder models, is a heavy-duty 4-speed that has a non-synchro first gear. This Warner T-18 unit has a super-low first gear ratio of 4.02:1 that makes it practically useless on a surfaced street but once off in the boondocks it proved to be a handy gear to have. As yet no automatic transmission is offered by Jeep but hopefully this improvement will follow shortly, perhaps by next year. Another change in the power train system is a Dana 20 transfer case with a low range ratio of 2.03:1 which replaces the old-style 2.46:1 ratio of earlier days. Shifting into and out of 4WD is a simple thing with the Dana transfer case, particularly when the vehicle is equipped with locking front hubs as our three test cars were.

The wealth of improvements on the new Jeep CJ-5s extends also to the running gear. Up front there is a new axle, the Dana 30 replacing the Dana 27, which increases wheel track from 48.4 inches to 51.5 inches but that is not its primary function. The new axle's

))))

Out Front

main purpose for being on the car is its open-end balljoint configuration, a trick picked up from the Chevrolet K/5 Blazer, that has a greater turning angle and also reduces the overall turning circle to a miniscule 32.9 feet from the former 35.0 feet. A new rear axle is also included in the CJ-5 this year and has an increased track over former models and a 3,000-lb. capacity rather than the older 2,500-lb. rating. Different axle ratios are available with the new engines, the standard being a 3.73:1 gear, which we had on the V8 test model, and an optional 4.27:1 ratio included with the two 6 cylinder test cars.

When we tested the 1971 CJ-5, one of our primary complaints was with the vehicle's manual steering that required untold amounts of muscle strain to operate. For 1972, Jeep has gone to a recirculating ball steering system, doing away with the old cam-and-lever arrangement. An added bonus to this new setup is fewer steering joints incorporated in the assemblage making servicing much easier and acting to reduce free play when parts start to wear. The recirculating ball unit has a slower ratio than before, 24:1, that measurably decreases wheel effort but, likewise, increases the required amount of wheel turning. However, a major advance has been made in this area with availability of a Saginaw power steering system as an option. This new offering has a ratio of 17.5:1 and makes the 1972 Jeeps much easier to maneuver, which is important when you are guiding the vehicles between rocks and trees.

Another complaint we had with last year's Jeep was woefully inadequate manual brakes. Now, if you order the V8 engine option, you can also get power assisted 4-wheel drums that, while quite touchy to any pedal pressure, really stop the vehicle and do so again and again without fail. Even if you don't get the power option, the drums have been enlarged, from 10-inch diameter to 11 inches, for a total effective lining area of 180.8 square inches; more than enough to provide adequate braking performance.

In the area of suspension little has been done except to bolster the front springs' capacity to handle the added weight of the heavier engines, although this has been accomplished without alternating the payload rating of the vehicle. The longitudinally-mounted leaf springs now have a ground rating of 1,015 lbs. In the rear, the leaf springs retain last year's rating of 1,405 lbs. If you want it, there is also an optional heavy-duty GVW package which provides front springs rated at 1,460 lbs. and 1,425-lb. rear springs plus heavy-duty shock absorbers and rugged 6.00 x 16 6-ply rated tires. We had our V8-equipped test vehicle ordered with this option while the two 6 cylinder models came with the standard suspension components and H78x15 tires.

One of the prime design concepts of the original military Jeep was to make an all-purpose vehicle that was as small and light as possible. Through the years the Jeep has never lost this basic aim, changing its size very little. Now, however, AMC has tampered with the idea but only enough to fit in the new equipment just made available. In addition to the increased front and rear tracks that have resulted in a wider, 71.7-inch, vehicle, the Jeep's rugged 6-crossmember frame has been lengthened and the wheelbase increased to 84 inches from its former 81 inches so that the larger engines could be dropped in. With the longer wheelbase, overall length is also upped more than 3 inches to 138.9 inches. This has been done, however, with only an 86-lb. increase in curb weight to 2,437 lbs., scarcely 200 lbs. more than the first Jeep built by Bantam before World War II.

With all of these changes you'd expect the new Jeeps to be different and they most definitely are. Our three test vehicles were equipped so that we could evaluate as many of the improvements and options as possible. The V8 model came with the top line equipment which included all available power equipment, the heavy-duty GVW package, a fixed tailgate, vinyl folding top, 3-speed transmission and front-mounted power winch. The 258 c.i. 6-cylinder car had the standard suspension, power steering, 4-speed transmission, fixed tailgate, power winch and full metal cab while the 232 c.i. vehicle was equipped with power steering, 4-speed transmission, fixed tailgate, standard springing and vinyl folding top. All three cars had heavy-duty alternators and batteries, heavy-duty frames, fuel tank and transfer case skid plates, sun visors, cigar lighter and dealer-installed roll bars and spare gasoline carriers.

Before getting into a driving impres-

sions description, it is best to understand from the outset that what faults the Jeep has are inherent in a vehicle as basic as this is and, in fact, lend a certain amount of primitive charm to the car and make it enjoyable. With either the vinyl top or metal cab on, a Jeep is hard to get into and out of and vision is restricted, especially to the rear and sides. The bare metal floor heats up to such an extent that you almost have to wear desert boots to bear the pain. The highway ride is harsh even with the standard suspension and tire noise blocks any sounds that may be emanating from the optional ratio. The cloth top flaps in the breeze and its plastic windows yellow with age and too many washings while the metal cab rattles and bangs until you think you're driving a tin can. Cargo room is sparse unless you don't buy the optional rear seat, at which point any extra passengers must find security by white-knuckling it on the roll bar. If you wish to play open roadster with the CJ-5, the erecting and dissassembling of the folding top will tax your knowledge even if you have owned an English sports car. But, as we said, these are things you expect with a Jeep. You don't buy one if you're after luxury and the finer things of life. You live with the shortcomings and enjoy to the limit the advantages of driving a Jeep in rough terrain.

The first thing you discover about driving a Jeep is the incredible amount of engine and fan noise which filters into the cab through the floorboards. It is disconcerting until you convince yourself that the engine isn't about to rupture itself and even wants to be revved higher. Once you've grown used to this, cruising down the freeway at speeds which can approach 90 mph is fairly easy although any wind gusts make you extra alert without much warning. The second thing you learn about a Jeep is how great it is off the road.

With the new line of engines, the 1972 CJ-5 is a real performer; no hill seems too high to climb and no rock, of moderate size, will deter it from its destination. The 304 V8 is, naturally enough, the best of the lot. It gives the Jeep new speed over rough land and makes climbing hills an enjoyable experience rather than a heart-rending disappointment. If the engine has one fault it is that it can get the immoderate driver into trouble all too quickly. The torque comes in at just the right point and, when in 4WD, bouncing along even the most rugged of trails can be accomplished in high gear. Although some off-roaders will object to the current trend towards larger engines in 4WD vehicles, in the Jeep the V8 is one of the best things to happen in years. The two 6-cylinder power plants also have plenty of off-road guts but do definitely need that super low first gear of the 4-speed transmission to make it up the steeper hills. Still, they both propel the CJ-5 over terrain at speeds that you would not believe. Of the two smaller engines, we prefer the 258 c.i. unit although the standard 232 c.i. motor more than makes up for the old in-line 4-cylinder it replaces.

Riding in the new Jeeps under off-

››››

Left: Powered by American Motors engines, the 1972 Jeeps become real performers. Above: In addition to the normal vinyl and cloth top, Jeeps are available with metal full cabs which keep out the elements but rattle incessantly. Below: The dashboard of a Jeep is pure utility with one centrally located dial. However, new this year are optional oil and amp gauges.

Out Front

road conditions is more bearable than in the past since the longer wheelbase does tend to ever-so-slightly smooth things out. Still, you can find yourself haphazardly flying over washboard-type surfaces if you aren't careful, with your head alternately shoved through the cab top or pounded into the shoulder blades. The seats, while more comfortable in the previous models due to a well-padded full-foam construction, do not provide the needed support for the lower back when really rugged going is encountered. Lateral support is better than before, although seat belts are a must to keep you behind the wheel. In our test we found some roads that would thoroughly pound the suspension and, despite the fact that the heavier engines take up most of the suspension travel, yet we never once bottomed anything and the 8.5-inch ground clearance (9.5 inches with the 16-inch wheels) proved sufficient to escape even the hairiest of rocks and ruts with nary a scratch on the skid plates.

Maneuverability has always been good with a Jeep but with the new power steering, open-end front axle and power brakes the CJ-5 is more nimble than ever. The fast and light steering makes avoiding obstacles extremely easy and greatly saves on arm fatigue. There is virtually no slop in the Saginaw unit as the wheels deflect the instant you turn the steering wheel. The power assisted brakes are a bit touchy but the boost is proper and the overriding sensation is one of being able to stop almost instantaneously. The standard brakes, while good, take quite a bit of pedal effort and require the driver to look far down the road for any unexpected problems since the stopping, or at least slowing, distance is much greater than with the power unit. Hopefully Jeep will see fit to offer power brakes as an option on all models in the future. We wouldn't want to be without it.

At the end of our test we were all impressed with the 1972 Jeep CJ-5s. They had performed flawlessly and exhibited an uninhibited exuberance for off-road punishment that had somehow been lacking before. If we were to rank them according to the competition, the new Jeeps would fit in just ahead of the Land Cruiser, if equipped with the V8 option, or just behind the Toyota vehicle if powered by one of the two 6-cylinder engines. The Chevy Blazer remains out of reach but this is not surprising since it occupies a different segment of the off-road market. In all, this is good news to the off-roader since every-now-and-then the Grandfather has to show his kids something. /MT

Although looking much the same as before, the Jeep is now 3 inches longer and almost 2 inches wider. Front winch, roll bar, and spare gas can carriers are worthwhile dealer options.

SPECIFICATIONS	V8 JEEP CJ-5	258 c.i. JEEP CJ-5	232 c.i. JEEP CJ-5
Engine	90° V8 OHV	6-Cyl. in-line OHV	6-Cyl. in-line OHV
Bore & Stroke — ins.	3.75 x 3.44	3.75 x 3.90	3.75 x 3.50
Displacement — cu.in.	304	258	232
HP @ RPM	150 @ 4200	110 @ 3500	100 @ 3600
Torque: lbs.-ft. @ rpm	245 @ 2500	195 @ 2000	185 @ 1800
Compression Ratio	8.4:1	8.0:1	8.0:1
Carburetion	2 bbl.	1 bbl.	1 bbl.
Transmission	3-Speed manual	4-Speed manual	4-Speed manual
Final Drive Ratio	3.73:1	4.27:1	4.27:1
Steering Type	Recirculating ball	Recirculating ball	Recirculating ball
Steering Ratio	17.5:1	17.5:1	17.5:1
Turning Diameter (curb-to-curb-ft.)	32.9	32.9	32.9
Wheel Turns (lock-to-lock)	N.A.	N.A.	N.A.
Tire Size	6 00 x 16	H78 x 15	8.45 x 15
Brakes	Drum/drum	Drum/drum	Drum/drum
Front Suspension	Longitudinal leaf springs, shocks	Longitudinal leaf springs, shocks	Longitudinal leaf springs, shocks
Rear Suspension	Longitudinal leaf springs, shocks	Longitudinal leaf springs, shocks	Longitudinal leaf springs, shocks
Body/Frame Construction	Ladder frame, separate steel body	Ladder frame, separate steel body	Ladder frame, separate steel body
Wheelbase — ins.	84.0	84 0	84.0
Overall Length — ins.	138.9	138.9	138.9
Width — ins.	71.7	71.7	71.7
Height — ins.	69.5	69.5	69.5
Front Track — ins.	51.5	51.5	51.5
Rear Track — ins.	50.0	50.0	50.0
Curb Weight — lbs.	2,437	2,422	2,405
Fuel Capacity — gals	16.5	16.5	16.5
Oil Capacity — qts.	5	5	5
Ground Clearance — ins.	9.5	8.5	8.5
Approach Angle	45°	45°	45°
Departure Angle	30°	30°	30°
Gas Mileage Range — on road	8.2 — 13.4 mpg	8.0 — 12.6 mpg	11.8 — 14.7 mpg
Gas Mileage Range — off road	6.2 — 9.4 mpg	7.8 — 10.1 mpg	9.1 — 11.1 mpg
Base Price	$2,955.00	$2,955.00	$2,955.00
Price as Tested	$4,026.55	$4,407.10	$3,938.00
MT Road Test Score	72.8	71.0	70.2

Someone forgot to tell Gordon Rust that wildly painted and super-sanitary Jeeps are supposed to be kept on the pavement. Gordon's is a dual purpose machine; it serves as everyday transportation and on the weekends, he heads it for the back country.

At the time when most of the work was done on the Jeep, Gordon was service manager for Con-Ferr in Burbank, Calif., a four-wheel drive specialist shop. Seeing some of the customers' fantastic machines being prepared, like Steve McQueen's street and dirt jeeps, and many other off-road race cars, Gordon could not resist the urge to build his own. He started to work on his Jeep and it seemed to snowball into something that looks almost too good to ever be caught on the dirt.

Power for this hot rod style CJ3B machine is a stock high performance 289-cubic-inch Ford engine that formerly was one of the Cobra movers. Gordon felt it had plenty of power as is and wanted all the reliability he could get. No one needs a *plug* that lets you down 50 miles out in no-man's-land.

To shoehorn the engine swap, Gordon made up a new front crossmember using a piece of three-inch channel. The new piece gave six inches of added room up front over the old crossmember. The extra room was used for a larger radiator to keep the new Ford engine in a safe temperature range no matter what the driving conditions. A '49 Cad radiator was found to be just what was needed. It fit the space perfectly and is a heavy duty unit.

The transmission decided upon was the Borg Warner T-10 Ford full synchro four-speed unit, but it took lots of work to fit it in and retain the four-wheel-drive. The tail shaft had to be cut down, which required a new main shaft. Gordon's answer to *why not go to the supply house and get the kit that simplifies this swap,* was that his ten years' experience as a machinist and having access to the proper equipment, it seemed only right that he should make his own. He had been making parts for his friends' hot rods and boats, so now it was time to do his bit for himself.

Gordon's main problem with the Jeep has been driveshafts. Everytime he got on it in the sand, he broke a driveshaft. The car was an expert at twisting driveshafts. He solved this problem by making up a set of thick wall Chrome-Moly tube unit . Regular universal joints were used because Gordon felt it was much quicker and a whole lot cheaper to replace a U-joint than a driveshaft. U-joints can be repaired quickly. This way, if something happened, it did not spoil an entire outing, but rather took a few minutes underneath the car. Some of you Jeep owners with the same problem might like to try Gordon's idea.

Jeep offers suspension setups in light, medium, and heavy-duty. Gordon felt the way he drove and where he drove, made it wise to choose a super heavy-duty spring for the front and rear. The new spring he had made up has 14 leaves. He used the spring on all four corners and heavy-duty Monroe shocks. Warner Spring Co. of Los Angeles, Calif., made up the new springs.

The engine swap necessitated a new steering box setup. A '69 Chevelle steering gear and shaft was fitted and modified to fit the interior. A '65 Chevy steering column with the tilt wheel was modified to fit at a comfortable angle for the driver.

The wildest part of this Jeep is the paint job. Molly's Paint Studio was given the green light to do anything they wanted to. Aptly, the color scheme is Candy Lime Green and dark green. The blended colors were not enough to be outstanding so the leaf pattern was added to make it a one-of-a-kind. Over all this, Molly sprayed on a clear coating he uses on the fuel burning drag cars to protect their finish from the fuel. He knew Gordon's Jeep would get lots of off-road driving and felt it would add longer life

HOT ROD JEEP

Accessory gauges are Stewart-Warner. Square unit is an aircraft type compass. The '64 Chevy steering column sports an inlaid wood Coveco steering wheel.

Gordon's roll cage is a little different than most. Seats are stock Jeep units. Battery can be seen behind the front seat.

289 cubic-inch Ford fits quite well. It required a new front crossmember and motor mounts. A stock 750 cfm Holley four-barrel carb is used.

Business type roll cage is the only part of this Jeep that goes along with the surrounding terrain. Rust's Jeep looks as if it belongs in a car show instead of climbing hills and sand dunes.

CAN A SHOW CAR FIND HAPPINES IN THE DIRT

It's hard to believe this Jeep has seen a lot of off-road use and Gordon assures us he never babies the car in the dirt. He feels it was built to go anywhere and that's the way it is going to be driven.

to his labors. Proof of the pudding is that the car was painted over three years ago and has seen all the elements, sand, mud, rocks, dirt, etc., and still the paint is in mint condition.

The only noticeable modification to the body is the addition of the rear wheel-well extensions. A large truck fender was cut in half and each piece fitted inside the wheel well. Having the piece extend inside the well made them easier to fasten than using fiberglass units.

While at Con-Ferr, Gordon had fellow employee, Chuck Atkinson, build a sharp looking roll cage. He wanted something strong yet different looking than any of the other Jeeps running around the hills.

Gordon says there are still some changes upcoming for the dual-purpose machine. Shortly, the double roll bar is going to be covered with stainless steel sheeting and the steering changed over to a power unit. Also in the works is a dual spare tire rack and a stainless steel dash unit. We think its wild just the way it is.

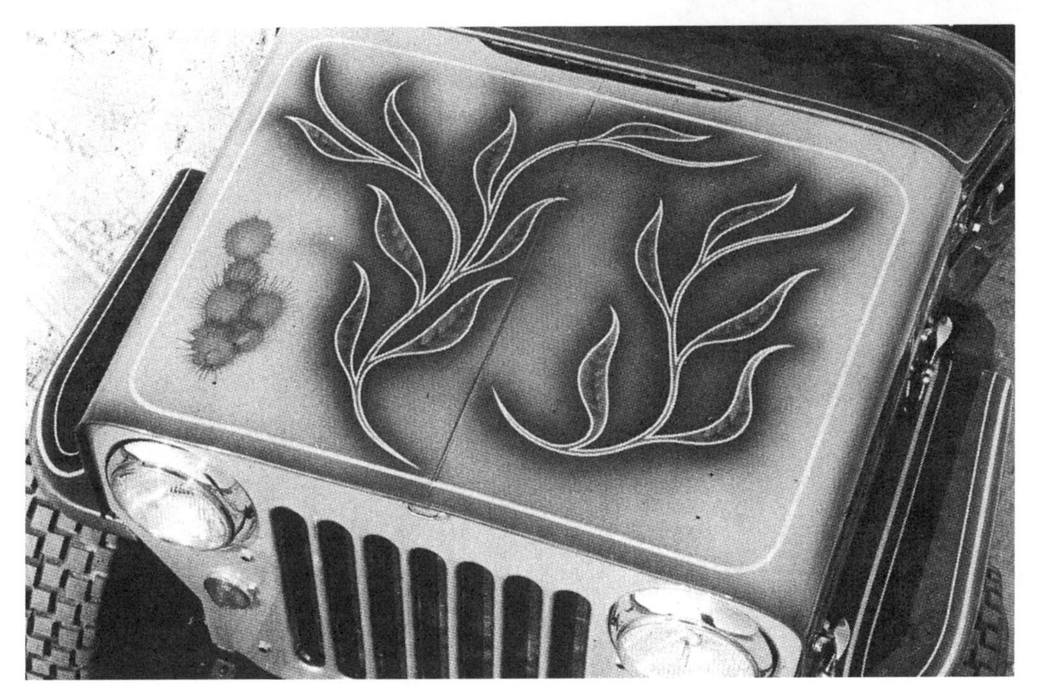

Grille section was painted *Silver Metalflake.* Bumper was made up from a piece of three-inch thick wall rectangular tubing with the ends filled in. Engine swap forced the steering box out front but gets the job done even so.

When Molly is turned loose he comes up with some wild paint ideas. Fuel clear was applied over all this madness to give the paint durability and to make it easy to clean after a long weekend on the dirt.

Jeep
UGX 97M

ROAD TEST

JEEP CJ-5

FOR : good performance from smooth, quiet engine ; versatile transmission easy to use ; goes anywhere (almost) ; runs on cheap fuel

AGAINST : unsatisfactory conversion to right-hand drive ; uncomfortable seats and driving position ; cramped accommodation ; poor weatherproofing and heater ; heavy clutch and brakes ; rather thirsty

It has taken 34 years for the Jeep to reach the UK. This institution on wheels has never before been on general sale to the British public the majority of existing immigrants being one-off imports or cast-offs left by departing Americans.

Born during the war, it was initially an uncompromising military vehicle from the wheels upwards, and by 1945 well over 600,000 of them were strewn around the world. Many of these are still in everyday use, for despite their torsionally flexible chassis and cheap four-cylinder engine, they were as tough as the boots that drove them.

The Jeep has since matured into a genuine multi-purpose civilian vehicle, the CJ5 tested here being more versatile, strong, quick and comfortable than its ancestors. For this reason the Jeep's new makers, American Motors Corporation have no qualms about pitting it against our own Land-Rover. Indeed, because of ever increasing sales of FWD vehicles and the continuing shortage of the Solihull product, AM visualise a flourishing market for their new import. The forecast is 5000 sales a year by 1977.

In some ways the modern Jeep is much better than its British counterpart. In terms of performance, for instance, the basic 3.8 litre American engine will outperform all but the much more expensive Range Rover. The handling, steering and ride are marginally better as well, and the gearing is more suitable for road work.

For those who require a long-lasting workhorse however, strength and durability will be more important faotors. Though our 1000-mile test is not sufficient for us to judge reliability or durability. In terms of finish, proteotion and for that matter equipment, the Jeep is inferior to the Land-Rover. There is no aluminium panelling or galvanised steel framework as on all Land-Rovers ; in fact rust was already appearing through the thin paintwork in several parts of our test car. Nor did we like the brakes or the conversion from left to right hand drive which is rather primitive. A simple steering wheel swop leaves the driver sitting on a bench seat with the gearlever and foot operated parking brake very badly positioned.

At £1572, the CJ5 (the CJ6 is a 104in LWB version) is already quite competitively priced in the UK—short wheelbase four-cylinder Land-Rovers start at £1308—so it will doubtless find a ready market here.

PERFORMANCE

The engine fitted to the imported CJ5 is an in-line six-cylinder ohv unit—V8 versions are available in the States. In its fully emissionised form it produces 100 bhp at 3500 rpm and a beefy 185 lb ft of torque very low in the range at 1800 rpm.

Momentarily flooring the accelerator will set the automatic choke for cold starting. However frosty the weather the engine then pulls strongly and without fuss. Once the choke cuts out, the engine assumes a steady, even tickover. In the absence of a rev counter maximum engine speed is determined more by a fall-off in power than any sound of mechanical strain.

Though 100 bhp is a very modest output from 3.8 litres, the Jeep's performance is quite adequate and certainly superior to that of the Land-Rover. Sixty mph comes up in just 14.3 seconds and the standing ¼ mile is covered in 19.2 seconds. This acceleration compares with cars like the Honda Civic and AlfaSud.

Top gear performance is much more impressive, the 30-50 mph time of 7.0 seconds matching that of the V8 Aston Martin. Though this flexibility is not so evident higher in the range, the incredible torque takes much of the strain out of town driving and the Jeep will actually start from rest in top and pull vigorously from as little as 10 mph.

Maximum speed, though perhaps a bit aoademic, is a useful 78.8 mph, rising to an unstressed 84.1 mph on our best flying quarter mile.

The excellent torque of the engine was particularly useful on the rough and we found the Jeep would pull itself out of craters and over ploughed fields in high-range at times when the Land-Rover would be begging for a lower gear.

Though producing a mere 100 bhp from 3.8 litres, the Jeep's conventional straight-six engine has an impressive amount of torque and is particularly smooth. Underbonnet accessibility is good and servicing should present no problems

ECONOMY

The fuel consumption of the Jeep's single carburetter engine is heavy by any standards. During our tenure the vehicle covered 1000 miles on the road, did some very rough terrain journeys and a day's testing at MIRA. For all this it gave 13.9 mpg, only two less than the computed touring consumption of 15.9. We doubt if many owners would do much better.

With its 12.9 gallon tank the Jeep will travel up to 205 miles between fill-ups. Despite an 8.0:1 compression ratio it runs happily on the 91 octane fuel available in this country. It will also stomach the lead-free variety.

TRANSMISSION

The Jeep has six forward ratios, two reverse gears and a choice of two- or four-wheel drive, yet the controls are remarkably straightforward. They also differ from those of the Land-Rover in two important respects: two rather than three levers operate the entire system and reversion to two-wheel drive can be accomplished on the move. With the Land-Rover it is necessary to stop first.

The main lever, due to the rather half-hearted RHD conversion, is angled away from the driver. However its movements are quite light and precise. The gears are set in the conventional H pattern, reverse occupying the upper left position.

A smaller lever to the right works the transfer box. Four-wheel drive high range is obtained very easily, by pushing the transfer lever forward—no clutch work is required for this operation. Working backwards towards the driver, there is a neutral position which can be selected at offs, and finally the low range position which can be selected at crawling speed.

For road driving first and second are comparatively low but then they obviously come into their own when driving on the rough. There is also a fair-sized gap between second and top, but this is no problem either because of the engine's exceptional torque. All told we thought the choice of ratios to be very good—better than those of the Land-Rover.

In almost any other vehicle, the heavy clutch with its badly placed pedal would become very tiresome. However, once again the engine's torque comes to the rescue as the amount of essential gearchanging is minimal, even around town.

Surprisingly, there's little transmission whine, even when in the four-wheel drive.

HANDLING

On the road the Saginaw recirculating ball steering is vague and low geared. On the rough, however, it copes admirably with ploughed fields, sodden cart tracks and grassy banks. Basically it is an acceptable compromise. The lock is not very good though, at 34ft 7in.

Whatever the handling characteristics of a vehicle, they tend to be emphasised by a particularly short wheelbase. Like the Land-Rover, if the Jeep does break away at the back it does so rather suddenly and calls for quick correction. This situation can occur quite easily on wet tarmac, and certainly on London streets after a shower, when the available torque is more than enough to break traction. Care is needed in the wet when making downward gear changes as it's all too easy to lock the wheels if engine and gearbox speeds are not properly matched.

Usually, selection of four-wheel drive seems to have virtually no effect on the weight of the steering, and the handling and roadholding are immediately improved by its use in slippery conditions. However, early reversion to rear-wheel drive is advised when on the road in the interest of tyre wear.

British models come equipped with 15in Goodyear Suburbanite tyres which seemed a fair compromise, though perhaps they were more at home on rough terrain than very wet tarmac.

Above: a half-hearted conversion from LHD to RHD results in the driver occupying the unadjustable bench seat. The gearlever is angled away rather than towards him. The driving position is poor

Left: accommodation is quite limited and length and width-wise less than most estate cars. The optional, substantial roll cage prevents the wheel-boxes being used as temporary seats

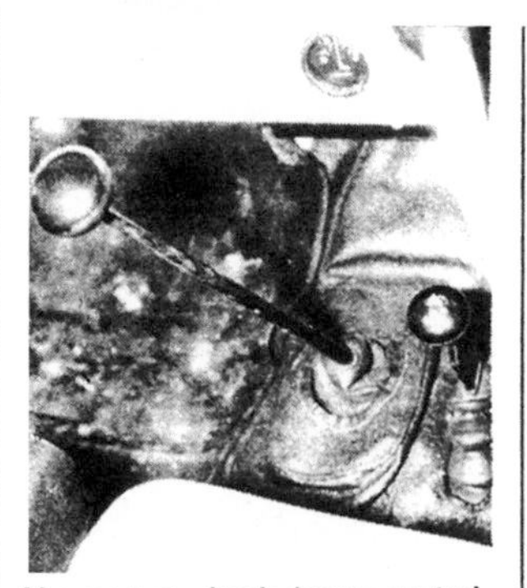

Above: two simple levers control the excellent multi-purpose transmission. Four-wheel drive can be engaged and disengaged on the move

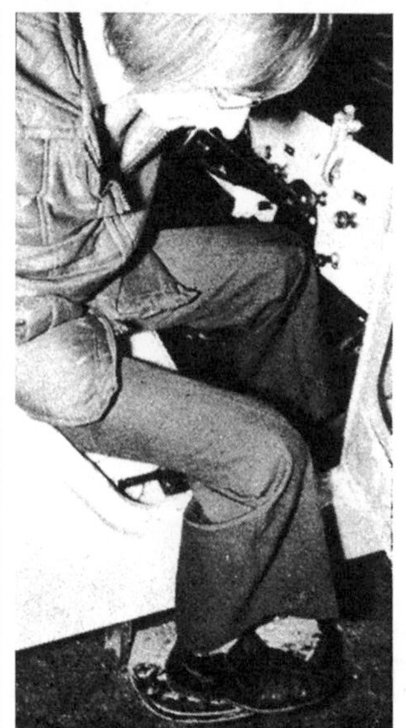

Right: exit and entry is quite awkward, especially from the driver's side, where the large wheel gets in the way

MOTOR ROAD TEST No. 6/74 • AMERICAN MOTORS JEEP CJ5

BRAKES

Four large servo-assisted drum brakes arrest the Jeep's substantial 26 cwt. As can be seen, a 25 lb pedal pressure has little effect, and even 100 lb produced no more than 0.811 g. This full emergency stop involved considerable weaving due to an apparent imbalance in the system. In the wet, this could have been tricky.

Rather than deteriorate, the brakes actually improved during our 20-stop fade test though a hint of instability was evident during these half-g stops. A thorough soaking in the watersplash had no effect whatsoever.

Although the foot-operated parking brake had ceased to work on the offside wheel we still managed a commendable 0.33 g stop from 30 mph. However, it failed to hold the car on anything greater than a 1 in 6 incline.

ACCOMMODATION

The CJ5 has a very short (84in) wheelbase—four inches shorter than the comparable Land-Rover for instance. This leaves a mere 40in of loading space between the seats and the tail, considerably less than in most modern estate cars. Loading heavy objects is hampered by the height of the drop-down tailgate, though objects up to 3ft wide can be accommodated between the narrow wheelboxes.

Oddments can be stowed together with the tools in the hatch under the driver's seat and there is room for maps and papers in the large door pockets. There is no parcel shelf.

Though there's sufficient space for three passengers in the front, anybody sitting on the bench seat with the driver tends to tangle with the gear lever. Without the added bulk of the optional roll-cage there is temporary accommodation for another four people on the wheelboxes in the back.

The Jeep will carry up to 1300 lb as well as three passengers and as a tow vehicle will cope with 3750 lb. If you want more space the CJ6 has a 104 in wheelbase and will take a slightly heavier load.

RIDE COMFORT

Without the use of variable rate suspension it is difficult to provide such a short wheelbase vehicle with a decent unladen ride. Even so, that of the leaf-sprung Jeep is acceptable if poor by car standards. Around town it is harsh and rather jerky though free of bangs and crashes. On smooth main roads it rides quite well.

AT THE WHEEL

Several aspects of the very poor driving position are attributable to the RHD conversion. To start with, instead of sitting on the single seat made for the job, you now have to occupy half of the bench seat—this can't be changed because of

PERFORMANCE

CONDITIONS

Weather	Drizzle, wind 10-15 mph
Temperature	44-48° F
Barometer	29.0 in. Hg
Surface	Damp tarmac

MAXIMUM SPEEDS

	mph	kph
Banked circuit	78.8	126.8
Best ¼ mile	84.1	135.3
Terminal speeds:		
at ¼ mile	70	113
at kilometre	78	126
Speed in gears (at 4500 rpm):		
1st	30	
2nd	57	

ACCELERATION FROM REST

mph	sec	kph	sec
0-30	4.2	0-20	1.3
0-40	6.4	0-40	2.9
0-50	9.9	0-60	5.8
0-60	14.3	0-80	9.8
0-70	21.2	0-100	15.6
		0-120	28.0
Stand'g ¼	19.2	Stand'g km	37.6

ACCELERATION IN TOP

mph	sec	kph	sec
20-40	6.4	40-60	4.1
30-50	7.0	60-80	4.3
40-60	8.3	80-100	6.0
50-70	11.5	100-120	12.3

FUEL CONSUMPTION

Touring*	15.9 mpg 17.8 litres/100 km

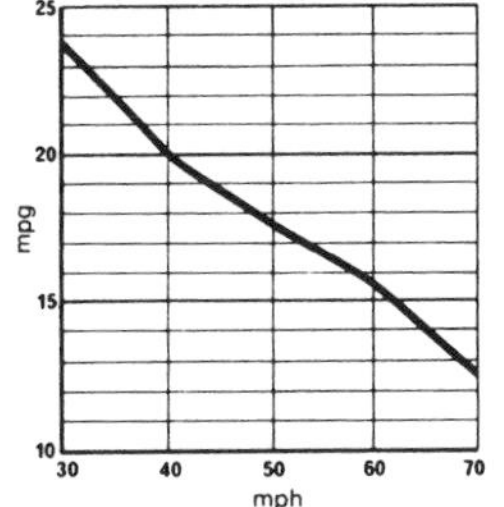

Overall	13.9 mpg 20.3 litres/100 km
Fuel grade	91 octane (RM) 2 star rating
Tank capacity	12.9 galls 58.6 litres
Max range	205 miles 330 km
Test distance	1050 miles 1689 km

* Consumption midway between 30 mph and maximum less 5 per cent for acceleration.

BRAKES

lb	kg	g	ft	m
25	11	0.09	333	102
50	23	0.49	61	19
60	27	0.59	51	16
65	30	0.68	44	13
100	45	0.81	37	11
Handbrake		0.33	91	28

FADE

20 ½g stops at 1 m intervals from speed midway between 40 mph (64 kph) and maximum (59 mph, 95 kph)

	lb	kg
Pedal force at start	60	27
Pedal force at 10th stop	55	25
Pedal force at 20th stop	50	23

STEERING

Turning circle between kerbs	ft	m
left	35.6	10.9
right	33.9	10.3
Lock to lock		4.0 turns
50 ft diam circle		1.2 turns

CLUTCH

	in	cm
Free pedal movement	2.0	5.1
Additional to disengage	3.5	8.9
Maximum pedal load	70 lb	32 kg

SPEEDOMETER (mph)

Speedo	30	40	50	60	70
True mph	28	37.5	47	56	65

Distance recorder: 0.7 per cent fast.

WEIGHT

	cwt	kg
Unladen weight*	26.2	1331
Weight as tested	29.9	1519

* with fuel for approx 50 miles.

Performance tests carried out by Motor's staff at the Motor Industry Research Association proving ground, Lindley.

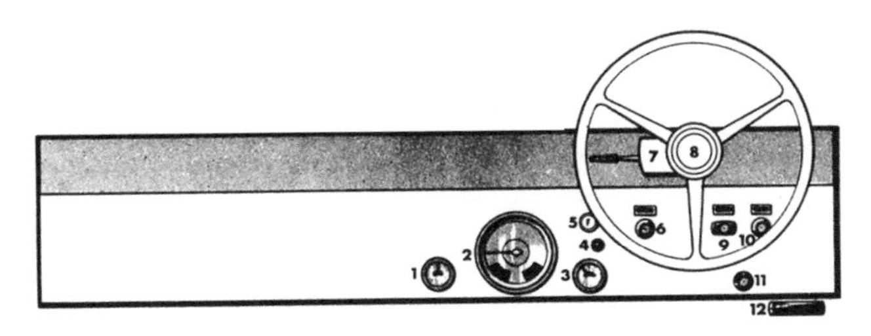

1 ammeter
2 speedometer/fuel and temperature gauge
3 oil pressure gauge
4 heater temperature control
5 ignition
6 hazard lights
7 indicators
8 horn button
9 wash/wipe switch
10 lights
11 heater blower
12 parking brake release

MOTOR ROAD TEST No. 6/74 • AMERICAN MOTORS JEEP CJ5

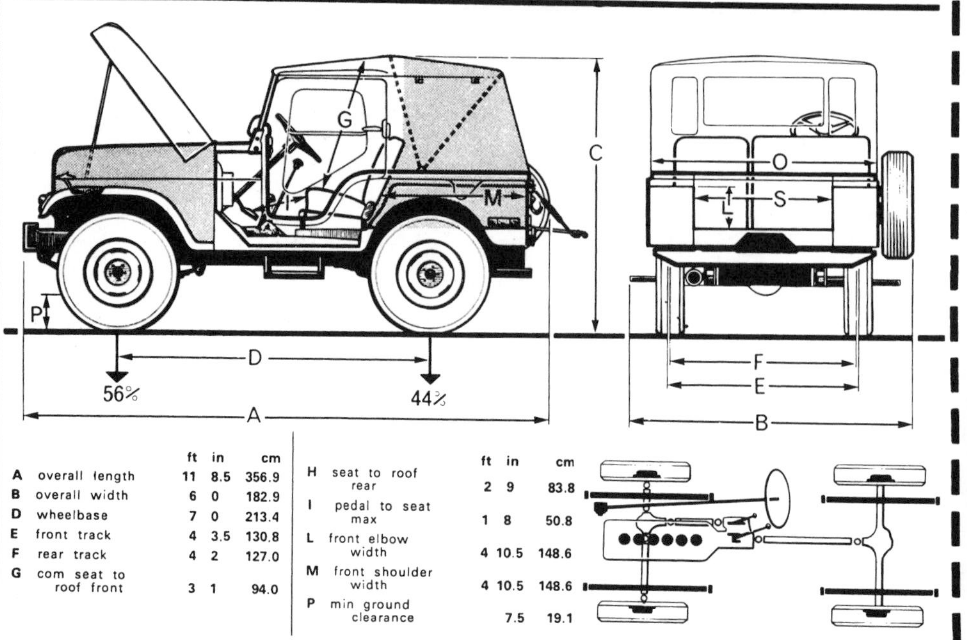

		ft	in	cm
A	overall length	11	8.5	356.9
B	overall width	6	0	182.9
D	wheelbase	7	0	213.4
E	front track	4	3.5	130.8
F	rear track	4	2	127.0
G	com seat to roof front	3	1	94.0
H	seat to roof rear	2	9	83.8
I	pedal to seat max	1	8	50.8
L	front elbow width	4	10.5	148.6
M	front shoulder width	4	10.5	148.6
P	min ground clearance		7.5	19.1

GENERAL SPECIFICATION

ENGINE

Cylinders	6 in line
Capacity	3803 cc (232 cu in)
Bore/stroke	95.3/88.9 mm (3.75/3.50 in)
Cooling	Water
Block	Cast iron
Head	Cast iron
Valves	Ohv
Valve timing	
inlet opens	12° btdc
inlet closes	66° abdc
ex opens	53° bbdc
ex closes	5° atdc
Compression	8.0 : 1
Carburetter	American Motors 6401S
Bearings	Seven main
Fuel pump	Mechanical
Max power	100 bhp (DIN) at 3600 rpm
Max torque	185 lb ft (DIN) at 1800 rpm

TRANSMISSION

Type	3-speed manual, high and low range, 2 or 4 wheel drive	
Clutch	10.5 in dia, sdp coil spring	
Internal ratios and mph/1000 rpm		
Top	1.00 : 1/20.4	1.00 : 1 /10.0
2nd	1.61 : 1/12.7	1.61 : 1/ 6.3
1st	3.10 : 1/ 6.6	3.10 : 1/ 3.3
Rev	3.10 : 1	3.10 : 1
Final drive	Spiral bevel 3.73 : 1	

BODY/CHASSIS

Construction	Unitary, all steel
Protection	Full underseal

SUSPENSION

Front	Longitudinal, multi-leaf, semi-elliptical springs, double-acting lever dampers
Rear	Longitudinal multi-leaf, semi-elliptical springs, double-acting lever dampers

STEERING

Type	Recirculating ball
Assistance	None
Toe-in	3/64-3/32 in
Camber	1.5°
Castor	3°

BRAKES

Type	Drums front and rear
Servo	None
Circuit	Split front and rear with tandem master cylinder
Rear valve	None
Adjustment	Self-adjusting

WHEELS

Type	Steel disc 15in x 6L
Tyres	Goodyear Suburbanite E78
Pressures	F 24; R 24 normal, F 28; R 28 max load

ELECTRICAL

Battery	12 volt 50Ah
Polarity	Negative earth
Generator	Alternator
Fuses	6
Headlights	2 sealed beam 40/50 W

STANDARD EQUIPMENT

Adjustable steering	No
Anti-lock brakes	No
Armrests	No
Ashtrays	No
Breakaway mirror	No
Cigar lighter	No
Childproof locks	No
Clock	No
Coat hooks	No
Dual circuit brakes	Yes
Electric windows	No
Energy absorb steering col	No
Fresh air ventilation	No
Grab handles	No
Head restraints	No
Heated rear window	No
Laminated screen	No
Lights	
Boot	No
Courtesy	No
Engine bay	No
Hazard warning	Yes
Map reading	No
Reversing	No
Spot/fog	No
Locker	No
Outside mirror	Yes
Parcel shelf	No
Petrol filler lock	No
Radio	No
Rev counter	No
Seat belts	
Front	Yes
Rear	No
Seat recline	No
Seat height adjuster	No
Sliding roof	No
Tinted glass	No
Combination wash/wipe	Yes
Wipe delay	No
Vanity mirror	No

IN SERVICE

GUARANTEE

Duration	12 months or 12,000 miles

MAINTENANCE

Schedule	Every 5000 miles
Free service	At 1000 miles

DO-IT-YOURSELF

Sump	**10 pints, SAE 30**
Gearbox	**5 pints, SAE 30**
Rear axle	**2.5 pints, SAE 30**
Coolant	**17.4 pints**
Contact breaker gap	**0.016 in**
Spark plug type	**Champion N127**
Spark plug gap	**0.033-0.037 in**
Tappets	**Hydraulic lifters**

REPLACEMENT COSTS

Clutch unit	**£37.52**
Complete exhaust system	**£13.35**
Engine (new)	**£304.90**
Damper (front)	**£4.52**
Front wing	**£20.47**
Gearbox (new)	**£153.16**
Oil filter	**£1.57**
Starter motor	**£30.93**
Windscreen	**£24.30**

Make: Jeep
Model: CJ5
Makers: American Motors Corporation, 14250 Plymouth Road, Detroit, Michigan 48232.
Concessionaires: American Motors Corporation (Great Britain) Ltd, Chiswick Flyover, Great West Road, London, W4 5QR
Price: £1429.00 plus £142.90 VAT equals £1571.90. Plus rear tow bar, £15.40; roll-cage, £29.70; rear tyre carrier, £34.10; and electric winch, £315.70 gives total as tested of £1966.80

the large hatch in the floor. Apart from it having no lateral support, you can't tailor the driving position in any way. Couple to these shortcomings a small cushion with poor thigh support, heavy offset pedals set far too high in the air, and an oversize steering wheel that is unnervingly close to your chest, and you'll understand why the Jeep is not very comfortable.

The major switches are symmetrically laid out, but are set too low on the facia and many of them are impossible to reach when wearing the seat belt. The gearlever also suffers from the

We found the pedals too high. Also the clutch is too heavy, the throttle too low and the parking brake almost unmanageable

conversion as it's angled away from the driver. Worst of all, however, is the foot-operated parking brake which, due to its relocation, now requires the attention of the driver's right foot. Trying to hold the vehicle on a steep hill while operating the parking brake with what would normally be one's "foot-brake foot" is difficult and dangerous.

The single stalk is for the indicators; the horn button is in the centre of the steering wheel.

VISIBILITY

Even in dry weather the slightly opaque side-windows give distracting reflections. In the wet the combination of water droplets hanging on the Perspex and the large unswept areas of the windscreen seriously reduce vision. Though restricted in movement the wipers clean effectively and the powerful electric washer is also good.

The inboard mounted headlights are no more than adequate.

INSTRUMENTS

Like the switches, the three gauges are set too low for easy reading, though they are well calibrated. A large circular speedometer with inset fuel and temperature gauges is sandwiched by an ammeter on the left and oil pressure gauge on the right.

Both the gauges and the switch tags are clearly illuminated by green lighting at night.

HEATING

Even at full blast the heater only successfully combats the incoming

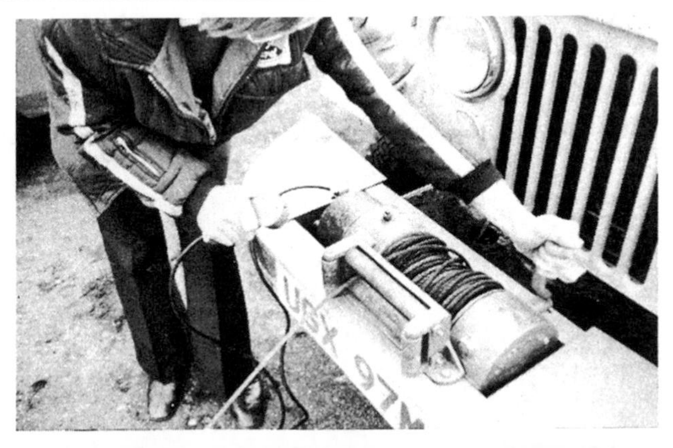

Top: the Ramsey electric winch is an extra £316. Above: the instruments and switches are well below the driver's sight line. The dipswitch is found between the clutch and brake pedals

draughts up to about 45 mph. Above that speed it loses the battle.

The controls are straightforward —a rheostat for the blower on the right of the facia, a knob for the water valve to the left of the steering column and flap valves at the base of the heater to determine the direction of flow.

In fact even with them closed, virtually no heat finds its way to the screen for defrosting.

VENTILATION

Apart from shutting the water valve so cold air is blown from the base of the heater, the only other ventilation in the Jeep comes from the draughts.

NOISE

Considering its structure and design the Jeep is really surprisingly quiet. Engine noise rarely rises to more than a distant and pleasant hum. Road noise is certainly noticeable but not as bad as one might expect, the tyres "singing" on coarse surfaces but remaining quiet on others. The greatest disturber of the peace is the wind. This rises from mild buffeting round the screen at low speed to a hood rippling racket at near maximum.

EQUIPMENT

As sold in the UK, the CJ5 comes complete with undercoated body, heater and the full soft top. There is also a list of useful optional extras: included on our test car were the rear tow bar, £15.40; roll-cage, £29.70, rear type carrier, £34.10, and electric winch, £315.70.

This device, made by the Ramsey Winch company, has a detachable remote control box and is sunk into the special extra-wide front umper. Drive is engaged by way of the large lever on the back of the winch itself.

FINISH

The Jeep's trim is deliberately and unashamedly basic. Rubber mats cover the floor of the cab, but everywhere else is painted metal. The seats are covered in vinyl cloth and the simple doors consist of a tough plastic covering over a rather flimsy steel frame. The hood is made of similar material and although fairly waterproof is difficult to refit, especially at the rear where there is a row of poppers.

Rust was beginning to form on the facia where rain had run from under the bottom of the screen; it also marred several outside areas. The basic lever-type door handles repeatedly came loose and were damaging the hood where they had rubbed against the door pillar. Generally the standard of finish is poor.

Above: the optional wheel holder swings back to allow access to the drop-down tail gate. Below: the doors have unzippable windows, but we found the frames weak and the handles self-loosening

IN SERVICE

Time will tell what the UK Jeep service is like, but AMC assure us that as Britain is to be used as the base for their activities in the Common Market, customers here will get first class service. Already dealerships have been set up and fitters trained in a special service school. There are also large stocks of spares allocated to the dealers and backed by a central supply at AM, Chiswick.

Either way servicing the Jeep should be no real problem. Under-bonnet accessibility is good, with most of the components needing regular attention within easy reach.

The basic toolkit, consisting of jack and wheelbrace, is kept in the locker under the driver's seat. The spare wheel itself is always mounted outside, usually on the rear offside wing; in our case on the optional carrier at the rear.

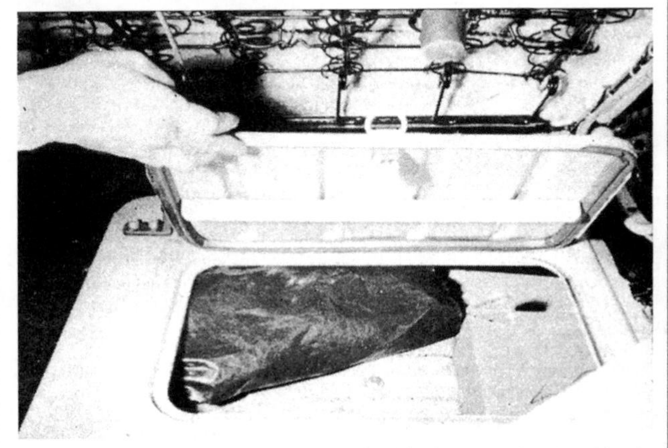

Above: the sparse tool kit is stored in this hatch under the driver's seat. Below left: the kit itself with the remote control for the electric winch. Below right: rust and flaking paint were noticeable at several points around the body

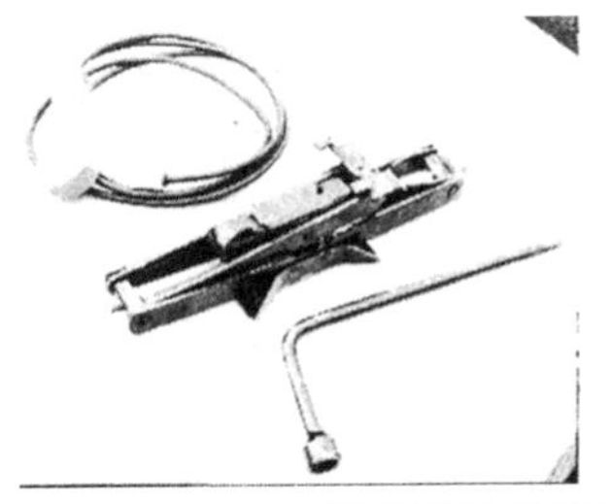

The Jeep®.
It has a lot of pull
in the right places.
NJ 8293 AU
It packs all the power you need, because it's got Jeep guts.
This baby is better than ever. And that's saying a lot, because the Jeep classic is the one people think of when it comes to multi-purpose 4-wheel drive vehicles.
To start with, open the hood. Inside are the biggest engines the Jeep has ever had. Powerful 6's. Or a mighty V-8. And look at the front axle. It's newly designed for greater maneuverability. Shortens the turning circle diameter by nearly six feet.
16.5' TURNING RADIUS
The steering mechanism is new on the hard-working Jeep, too. It requires less effort. And you can make it nearly effortless by adding power steering. And, naturally, you've got the world's most famous 4-wheel drive, so you go just about anyplace for the fun of it.
If you take your towing seriously, the Jeep offers such options as heavy-duty electrical and cooling systems, Trac-Lok differential, select drive front hubs and 4-speed transmission, to say nothing of trailer hitches.
Put it all together. See your Jeep dealer. It's the right place to pull off a great deal.
Toughest 4-letter word on wheels.
Jeep
Drive your Jeep vehicle with care and keep America the Beautiful.

JEEP CJ-5 VS. TOYOTA LAND CRUISER

PV4 COMPARISON TEST

WE TESTED THE TWO MOST POPULAR SMALL 4-WHEEL DRIVES SIDE BY SIDE

WHEN SETTING OUT to do a comparison test of vehicles there is always the feeling that no matter what you say you are going to alienate a large segment of people. However, comparison tests are very worthwhile in that the reader is able to see how two vehicles stack up when put through the same test procedures at the same time and under the same conditions. Our philosophy here at PV4 is that every vehicle has its good and bad points and that just because we find fault with a particular truck doesn't mean that some other driver in a different location and with different terrain to deal with might not find it a great vehicle.

This test is concerned with the two most popular small 4-wheel-drive utility vehicles, the Jeep CJ-5 and the Toyota Land Cruiser. Both of these are outstanding vehicles in our opinion and there are certainly a lot of people who agree with us judging by the number of them that are seen on the highways and in the outback. Both vehicles are seen in nearly every off-pavement situation.

The CJ-5 is the standard by which all 4-wheel-drive vehicles have been measured over the years. It is the descendant of the World War II Jeep which started it all. For many years the Jeep was about the only practical 4-wheel-drive vehicle available for recreational purposes.

The Toyota Land Cruiser on the other hand, came to these shores in the 1960s and has made a considerable impact on the 4wd scene. Toyota has retained its no-nonsense approach to the Land Cruiser design since its inception and there are no frills. It is, however, both practical and functional.

When we began our comparison testing of these two vehicles, we drew up a list of 18 points for judgment and asked each staff member who drove the vehicles to rate them. The list covered such items as engine response, steering characteristics, maneuverability and so on. Each vehicle was

The CJ-5 presents a pretty picture in the wilds of Baja in a setting of Ocotillo, sand and rocks. The CJ-5 is at home.

Hood is taller on the Land Cruiser otherwise there is a strong resemblance between the two vehicles from this angle.

Jeep has a more contoured, sloping top whereas the Toyota is rather boxy. Toyota was more dust-free than the CJ-5.

given a rating from poor to excellent. A poor rating was good for one point and an excellent meant five points with various steps in between. We then totaled the points and arrived at very similar conclusions from all the test drivers. We'll get into that in more detail at the conclusion of the report. First, let's take a close look at each of the vehicles.

JEEP CJ-5

The CJ-5 is one of the smallest of the 4wds, smaller in fact than just about anything until you get down to the Suzuki Brute and Haflinger class. It sits on an 84-in. wheelbase and measures just 138.9 inches overall. The overall height is 69.5 inches and the width is 59.9, making it ideal for getting into the tight places where others fear to tread.

The standard engine is a 232-cu-in. inline 6-cylinder affair that nets 100 horsepower at 3600 rpm. In addition, there is a larger 258-cu-in. 6-cylinder engine available as an option with 110 net horsepower as well as a 304-cu-in. V-8. This last powerplant has 150 horsepower at 4200 rpm, according to the Jeep factory.

The standard transmission is a 3-speed manual. For additional money you have a choice of a 4-speed manual but only with the 6-cylinder engines. With the V-8 you only get the 3-speed. The 3-speed is all-synchromesh in the forward gears and the 4-speed is synchronized in the top three. Both the transmissions are coupled to the engine via a 10.5-in. diameter clutch. There are two final drive ratios available on the CJ-5, 3.73:1 and 4.27:1.

The Jeep features drum brakes at all four corners and these are not power assisted unless you want to pay extra for it. The suspension is non-exotic, with semi-elliptic leaf springs on a live axle at both front and rear. Heavy duty front and rear springs and shocks can be ordered as a package.

The '74 models are little changed from prior years. They are still the functional and no-frills vehicles they have always been. We should point out that in addition to the CJ-5 which we used for this test, Jeep still manufactures the longer wheelbase CJ-6 model which shares all of the same components except for its wheelbase and overall length. The Renegade, which is the more stylish CJ-5 model with the V-8, fancy paint and other goodies, is being made in greater numbers as a regular production model rather than a limited-edition vehicle as in the past.

With the Jeep you can order a choice of four different tops, ranging from a full metal one to a fabric top that only covers the front seats. The driver's seat is the only one included in the basic price and you have to pay extra for the passenger's bucket seat as well as the optional rear bench seat. Other extras include heavy-duty cooling system, assist bar, cigar lighter and swing-out rear tire carrier.

Our test model CJ-5 came equipped with the 258-cu-in. 6-cylinder engine, 4-speed transmission, 3.73:1 limited-slip

Shape of door on CJ-5 makes quick entry or exit rather difficult.

Door is large on Toyota but door frame hitting body is very noisy.

Land Cruiser crossing a stream in a remote area of Baja. Toyota handled well off pavement but seemed stiffer than previous models tested.

rear axle and the full fabric top. In addition, it carried the heavy-duty cooling system, heavy-duty battery, passenger bucket seat and rear bench, passenger assist bar, oil gauge and ammeter. The West Coast list price was $4244 without tax and license.

TOYOTA LAND CRUISER

For comparison purposes, our Land Cruiser test vehicle was also the fabric-topped model. It did not have any optional equipment. Neither of the test vehicles had the free-running front hubs nor a winch. The Land Cruiser has as standard equipment many of the features for which you pay extra in other 4-wheel-drive vehicles. We, of course, had the California model which for 1974 has the new 4-speed manual transmission. This feature will also be available in the rest of the U.S. as soon as production of the 4-spds is great enough to cover the entire production of Land Cruisers. At that time the 3-spd will be phased out of production. In California, the 4-spd is an "enforced option" that costs $85. When the 4-spd is available for the rest of the country it will be an "enforced option" of $100.

The Land Cruiser features a 236.7-cu-in. inline 6-cylinder engine with a net horsepower rating of 138. Other standard equipment on the Land Cruiser includes a roll bar in the soft top model, power-assisted brakes, steering stabilizer, skid plates for the oil pan, transmission and transfer case, front bucket seats and rear benches and a 2-speed transfer case. In addition, there is a full fabric top and the basic price is $3849, West Coast POE. Since our test model did not have any options other than the 4-speed transmission, the list price excluding tax and license was $3934.

The standard 3-speed transmission has synchromesh in the top two gears while the new 4-speed has it in all forward gears. Both transmissions have 1.00:1 ratios in their respective top gears and both are coupled to a 4.11:1 rear axle ratio.

The suspension of the Land Cruiser is essentially the same as the CJ-5, with semi-elliptic leaf springs on live axles. Also like the Jeep, the Toyota has drum brakes at all four corners, however, they are assisted via a vacuum booster.

The Land Cruiser is a bit larger than the Jeep with a 90-in. wheelbase and overall length of 152.4 inches. It is also taller and wider by more than six inches.

In terms of optional equipment which you can order for your Land Cruiser the list is quite brief. Free-running front hubs, power takeoff or electric winches and an AM radio are just about all that is available from the dealer. The Toyota philosophy is to build the Land Cruiser with nearly everything you need from the start.

TEST & IMPRESSIONS

One of the first things that struck us about both vehicles was the noise level. It was fairly high in both with the Jeep ➤

JEEP CJ-5

PRICES

Basic list, FOB Toledo
- CJ-5 .... $3150*
- CJ-6 .... $3245*

*Prices subject to change during 1974

Standard equipment: 232-cu-in. ohv inline 6-cyl engine, 3-spd manual transmission, driver bucket seat, 2-spd transfer case, 2-spd electric wiper/washers, F78 x 15B tires, backup lights

ENGINES

Standard .... 232-cu-in. ohv inline 6
Bore x stroke, in .... 3.75 x 3.50
Compression ratio 8.0:1
Net horsepower @ rpm .... 100 @ 3600
Net torque @ rpm, lb-ft .... 185 @ 1800
Type fuel required .... 91 octane

Optional 258-cu-in. ohv inline 6 .... $54
Bore x stroke, in .... 3.75 x 3.90
Compression ratio 8.0:1
Net horsepower @ rpm .... 110 @ 3500
Net torque @ rpm, lb-ft .... 195 @ 2000
Type fuel required .... 91 octane

Optional 304-cu-in. V-8 .... $126
Bore x stroke, in .... 3.75 x 3.44
Compression ratio 8.4:1
Net horsepower @ rpm .... 150 @ 4200
Net torque @ rpm, lb-ft .... 245 @ 2500
Type fuel required .... 91 octane

DRIVE TRAIN

Standard transmission .... 3-spd manual
Clutch dia., in 10.5
Transmission ratios:
- 3rd .... 1.00:1(6-cyl), 1.00:1(V-8)
- 2nd .... 1.74:1(6-cyl), 1.83:1(V-8)
- 1st .... 3.10:1(6-cyl), 2.99:1(V-8)

Synchromesh .... all forward gears

Optional 4-spd manual (available on CJ-5 with 6-cyl engine only) $107
Transmission ratios: 4th 1.00:1
- 3rd 1.41:1
- 2nd 2.41:1
- 1st 4.01:1

Synchromesh .... 2nd, 3rd & 4th gear

Rear axle type .... semi-floating hypoid
Final drive ratios .... 3.73:1 & 4.27:1
Overdrive .... none

Free-running front hubs $60
Limited slip differential $59

Transfer case 2-spd
Transfer case ratios .... 2.03:1 & 1.00:1

CHASSIS & BODY

Body/frame: ladder-type frame and separate steel body
Brakes (std): 11 x 2-in. drums, front and rear
Brake swept area, sq in 276
Swept area/ton (max load) 122
Power brakes $45

Steering type (std) .... recirculating ball
Steering ratio 24:1
Turns, lock to lock 3.5
Power steering ratio 17:1
Turning circle, ft: 32.9 (CJ-5), 37.6 (CJ-6)

Wheel size (std) .... 15 x 5.5
Optional wheel sizes .... none
Tire size (std) .... F78 x 15B
Optional tire sizes .... H78 x 15B

SUSPENSION

Front suspension: semi-elliptic leaf springs on live axle with tube shocks
Front axle capacity, lb 2200
Optional .... none

Rear suspension: semi-elliptic leaf springs on live axle with tube shocks
Rear axle capacity, lb 2700
Optional .... none

Additional suspension options: HD front & rear shocks and HD front & rear springs, $38

ACCOMMODATION

Standard seats .... driver's bucket seat
Optional seats: front passenger bucket seat, $72; rear bench seat, $89

Headroom, in 36.0
Pedal to seatback, max 39.5
Steering wheel to seatback, max 15.5
Seat to ground 36.5
Floor to ground 21.5

Heater & defroster .... std
Tinted glass .... none
Air conditioning .... none

Unobstructed load space (length x width x height) in.
Rear folded or removed .... 37 x 36 x 46
Tailgate (width x height) .... 37.2 x 15

INSTRUMENTATION

Instruments: 0-90-mph speedometer, 99,999.9-mi. odometer, fuel gauge, water temp
Warning lights: oil pressure, alternator, hazard warning
Optional: oil gauge and ammeter, $17

MAINTENANCE

Service intervals, normal use, miles:
- Oil change 6000
- Filter change 6000
- Chassis lube 6000
- Minor tuneup 12,000
- Major tuneup 24,000

Warranty, months/miles 12/12,000

GENERAL

Curb weight, lb (test model) 2900
GVW (max. laden weight) 3750 (CJ-5), 3900 (CJ-6)
Optional GVWs: 4500 (CJ-5), 4750 (CJ-6)
Wheelbase, in 84.0/104.0
Track, front/rear 51.5/50.0
Overall length 138.9/158.9
Overall height 69.5/68.3
Overall width 59.9
Overhang, front/rear 26.0/28.0
Approach angle, degrees 34
Departure angle 33

Ground clearances (test model):
- Front axle 12.8
- Rear axle 8.2
- Oil pan 9.0
- Transfer case 10.0
- Fuel tank 12.5
- Exhaust system (lowest point) 9.8

Fuel tank capacity (U.S. gal) 15.5
Auxiliary tank .... none

OTHER OPTIONS

Renegade pkg $775
HD cooling $26
HD battery $11
Assist bar $7
Cigar lighter $9
Swing-out rear tire carrier .... $45+labor
Full metal top .... $370(CJ-5), 430(CJ-6)
Half metal top .... $336+labor
Full fabric top .... $193+labor
Half fabric top .... $161+labor
Energy absorbing chrome bumpers $125

PERFORMANCE DATA

TEST MODEL

CJ-5, 258-cu-in. 6-cyl engine, 4-spd transmission, 3.73 limited slip rear axle, passenger seat, rear bench seat, HD cooling, passenger assist bar, HD battery, roll bar, oil gauge and ammeter, cigar lighter, H78 x 15 tires, full fabric top
West Coast list price $4244

ACCELERATION

Time to speed, sec:
- 0-30 mph 5.0
- 0-45 mph 10.1
- 0-60 mph 16.0
- 0-70 mph 23.5

Standing start, ¼-mile, sec 20.3
Speed at end, mph 66

SPEED IN GEARS

High range, 4th (3700 rpm) 74
- 3rd (4000 rpm) 63
- 2nd (4000 rpm) 35
- 1st (4000 rpm) 21

Low range, 4th (4000 rpm) 43
- 3rd (4000 rpm) 31
- 2nd (4000 rpm) 17
- 1st (4000 rpm) 10

BRAKE TESTS

Pedal pressure required for ½-g deceleration rate from 60 mph, lb 45
Stopping distance from 60 mph, ft 209.5
Fade: Percent increase in pedal pressure for 6 stops from 60 mph 44
Overall brake rating .... fair

INTERIOR NOISE

Idle in neutral, dBA 62
Maximum during acceleration 85
At steady 70-mph cruising speed 86

OFF PAVEMENT

Hillclimbing ability .... excellent
Maneuverability .... excellent
Turnaround capability .... excellent
Handling .... very good
Ride .... fair

GENERAL

Heater rating .... good
Defroster effectiveness .... fair
Wiper coverage .... good

FUEL CONSUMPTION

Normal driving, mpg 13.7
Off pavement 9.2
Range, normal driving, miles 212
Range, off pavement 143

TOYOTA LAND CRUISER

PRICES

Basic list, West Coast POE

Land Cruiser soft-top	$3849
Land Cruiser hard-top	$4209

Standard equipment: 236.7-cu-in. ohv inline 6-cyl engine, 3-spd manual transmission (4-spd manual Calif. only), roll bar, power brakes, steering stabilizer, skid plates on oil pan, transmission and transfer case, front bucket seats and rear bench seat, 2-spd transfer case

ENGINES

Standard	236.7-cu-in. ohv inline 6
Bore x stroke, in	3.54 x 4.00
Compression ratio	7.8:1
Net horsepower @ rpm	138 @ 4000
Net torque @ rpm, lb-ft	213 @ 2200
Type fuel required	91 octane

DRIVE TRAIN

Standard transmission	3-spd manual
Clutch dia., in	10.8
Transmission ratios: 3rd	1.00:1
2nd	1.69:1
1st	2.75:1
Synchromesh	2nd & 3rd gear
Optional 4-spd manual (std in Calif.)	$100
Transmission ratios: 4th	1.00:1
3rd	1.41:1
2nd	2.29:1
1st	3.55:1
Synchromesh	all forward gears
Rear axle type	semi-floating hypoid
Final drive ratio	4.11:1
Overdrive	none

Free-running front hubs: Manual $70, Automatic $97

Limited slip differential	none
Transfer case	2-spd

Transfer case ratios: 2.31 & 1.00:1 (with 3-spd trans), 1.99 & 1.00:1 (with 4-spd trans)

CHASSIS & BODY

Body/frame: ladder-type frame with separate steel body

Brakes (std): 11.4 x 2.25-in. drums front and rear

Brake swept area, sq in	322
Swept area/ton (max load)	143
Power brakes	std
Steering type (std)	recirculating ball
Steering ratio	variable 20.5/23.5:1
Turns, lock to lock	3.5
Power steering	none
Turning circle, ft	35
Wheel size (std)	15 x 5.5 JJ
Optional wheel sizes	none
Tire size (std)	7.60 x 15B
Optional tire sizes	none

SUSPENSION

Front suspension: Semi-elliptic leaf springs on live axle with tube shocks

Front axle capacity, lb	2500
Optional	none
Additional suspension options	none

ACCOMMODATION

Standard seats: front bucket seats, rear fold-up seats

Optional seats	none
Headroom, in	41.0
Pedal to seatback, max	40.0
Steering wheel to seatback, max	16.0
Seat to ground	35.5
Floor to ground	22.0
Heater & defroster	std
Tinted glass	none
Air conditioning	none

Unobstructed load space (length x width x height) in.

With seats in place	43.5 x 22 x 48.5
Rear folded or removed	43.5 x 41 x 48.5
Tailgate (width x height)	48 x 15.3

INSTRUMENTATION

Instruments: 0-100-mph speedometer, 99,999.9-mi. odometer, oil pressure fuel level, water temp, ammeter

Warning lights: hazard warning, brake system warning

Optional	none

MAINTENANCE

Service intervals, normal use, miles:

Oil change	6000
Filter change	6000
Chassis lube	6000
Minor tuneup	12,000
Major tuneup	24,000
Warranty, months/miles	12/12,000

GENERAL

Curb weight, lb (test model)	3560
GVW (max. laden weight)	4500
Optional GVWs	none
Wheelbase, in	90.0
Track, front/rear	55.3/55.1
Overall length	152.4

Overall height: 76.0 (hard-top), 76.8 (soft-top)

Overall width	65.6
Overhang, front/rear	26.5/34.0
Approach angle, degrees	32
Departure angle	30

Grand clearances (test model):

Front axle	8.0
Rear axle	8.0
Oil pan	13.5
Transfer case	11.0
Fuel tank	19.0
Exhaust system (lowest point)	10.0
Fuel tank capacity (U.S. gal)	16.4
Auxiliary tank	none

OTHER OPTIONS

PTO	$400.
Electric winch	$346
AM radio	$61

PERFORMANCE DATA

TEST MODEL

Land Cruiser soft-top, 4-spd manual transmission

West Coast list price	$3934

ACCELERATION

Time to speed, sec:

0-30 mph	5.7
0-45 mph	11.3
0-60 mph	19.9
Standing start, ¼-mile, sec	21.8
Speed at end, mph	61

SPEED IN GEARS

High range, 4th (3600 rpm)	71
3rd (4000 rpm)	58
2nd (4000 rpm)	36
1st (4000 rpm)	22
Low range, 4th (4000 rpm)	40
3rd (4000 rpm)	29
2nd (4000 rpm)	18
1st (4000 rpm)	11

BRAKE TESTS

Pedal pressure required for ½-g deceleration rate from 60 mph, lb	38
Stopping distance from 60 mph, ft	190
Fade: Percent increase in pedal pressure for 6 stops from 60 mph	44
Overall brake rating	very good

INTERIOR NOISE

Idle in neutral, dBa	66
Maximum during acceleration	86
At steady 70-mph cruising speed	89

OFF PAVEMENT

Hillclimbing ability	very good
Maneuverability	excellent
Turnaround capability	very good
Handling	very good
Ride	fair

GENERAL

Heater rating	very good
Defroster effectiveness	good
Wiper coverage	good

FUEL CONSUMPTION

Normal driving, mpg	12.2
Off pavement	8.8
Range, normal driving, miles	200
Range, off pavement	144

being just a shade quieter. At a steady 70-mph cruising speed the Jeep registered 86 decibels on the A scale while the Land Cruiser came in with 89. The fabric tops add quite a bit to the noise level, cracking and popping with the wind at high speeds.

The Land Cruiser was the first 4-speed released for testing in the U.S. and we were disappointed to discover that the gear ratio in fourth is the same 1.00:1 as in third gear in the 3-speed. We had hoped that it would be more of an overdrive ratio which would allow for easier freeway cruising on the way to the outback. However, the 4-speed is a distinct improvement as there is better spacing of the gears and first is good and low.

In our driving of the two vehicles around town after we first picked them up we immediately noticed that the CJ-5 is much quicker and more responsive. This was demonstrated objectively at Orange County International Raceway in our acceleration tests. The Jeep was able to motor to 60 mph from a standing start in just 16.0 seconds while the Toyota needed 19.9. This same ratio continued in the quarter-mile acceleration runs in which the Jeep was a second and a half faster through the traps at 66 mph versus 61 for the Land Cruiser.

The rear seat of the Jeep CJ-5 is rather on the small side and a bit difficult to climb into. We find the Jeep better without it.

The Toyota Land Cruiser features two opposing rear seats which fold up when you want to carry more gear than people.

In the area of braking ability, the positions were reversed, with the Toyota getting the nod for superior performance. The Land Cruiser negotiated the panic stop from 60 mph in 190 feet compared to 209.5 feet for the Jeep. The degree of pedal pressure for a ½-g stop was about the same and the amount of fade in the brakes during the six consecutive stops from 60 was dead even. However, subjectively, the Toyota felt very steady and sure in the braking while the CJ-5 had a tendency to lock up the rear wheels and want to go sideways, which can be a bit unnerving.

In our off-pavement tests at Saddleback Park in Tustin, Calif. we did not encounter any great surprises. For hillclimbing, we have thought all along that both the Land Cruiser and the CJ-5 are hard to beat. The superior power of the Jeep in relationship to the Toyota proved the difference and we were able to outclimb the Toyota with the CJ-5. The difference is not all that great, however, and both deserve high ratings in that department.

To add to our comparison, we decided to take an extended trip into Baja California with both vehicles and shoot the cover picture down there. We loaded up the vehicles and spent three days "jeeping" through the northern half of the peninsula. Both the Jeep and the Toyota showed similar strong points and the same weaknesses. Both were able to negotiate the roughest stretches and the narrowest passages without trouble. At the same time, the ride in both was not especially pleasant, with the CJ-5 being better than the Toyota, which was a surprise. It seems to us that the suspension on this Land Cruiser is the stiffest we have ever experienced on a Toyota. Each irregularity in the terrain seemed to be transmitted directly to the occupants. Whoop-de-doos were uncomfortable in both vehicles due to the short wheelbases and it was generally a relief to get out every now and then to rest.

The steering of the CJ-5 was unsettling, especially in the sand where the slightest lack of concentration would mean heading off in another direction almost instantly. The Toyota was better in this regard. However, it had an equally disturbing trait. Due to the smog and emissions control apparatus, the Land Cruiser would not reduce its rpm to idle level when you took your foot off the accelerator pedal. Thus, each time you approached a bump or rock at any speed, you were forced to put on the brake as well as engage the clutch in order to slow down. This became tiresome after a long day in the outback.

The Jeep (left) and the Toyota front bumpers both have room for winch installation if desired. Front springs go beyond body.

In terms of comfort off the road, the Land Cruiser gets the nod over the CJ-5. The seats are much more luxurious and give considerably more support. Also, the Toyota does not tend to suck in as much dust off the pavement as the Jeep. On the other hand, the access to the storage area from the rear through the fabric top is much more convenient in the Jeep which uses snaps rather than tie-downs to secure the top.

The Land Cruiser has considerably more space inside for hauling gear and people than the Jeep and we were hard pressed to get all of the stuff we normally take along on a camping trip into the CJ-5. Other small things we noticed were the excellent tool kit that comes in every Land Cruiser which we think is a great idea; the trap-door storage area under the passenger's seat in the CJ-5, which is handy for stowing all the ➤

Sitting on Diablo Dry Lake in Baja California, the Jeep and the Toyota both look at home. The picture graphically demonstrates the size difference between the two vehicles. The Land Cruiser has considerably more room behind the front seats for gear.

The Jeep CJ-5 that we tested was equipped with the 258-cu-in. 6-cylinder engine which exhibited good performance.

Under the hood, the Toyota seems to have less space. The 6-cylinder engine suffers badly from emission controls.

The interior layout of the CJ-5 is plain and simple. We find the centered instrument cluster a bit hard to read.

The Land Cruiser's bucket seats are among the best we have experienced and there is full instrumentation.

Rear seat must be removed from CJ-5 to obtain any degree of cargo space. Seat is fastened with spring loaded mechanism.

Land Cruiser has more storage space than CJ-5 and rear seats don't have to be removed—just folded up against the side.

Toyota at speed on the Diablo Dry Lake close to San Felipe, Baja California. Handling on the dry lake bed was good.

small things that normally rattle around on the floor during a trip and get under foot; the lack of an interior light in the Jeep which is aggravating when looking for something at night; and the irritating presence of a ridge right at knee level in the Toyota door which bores into the driver's leg after several hours. These are admittedly nitpicking items but they do make an impression on you after awhile.

In terms of fuel economy, there is little difference between the two in our experience. Both will average around 12 to 14 mpg on the pavement and about 8 to 10 off. These figures make for a somewhat limited range as the fuel tank capacities are not very great; 16.4 gallons in the Toyota and 15.5 in the CJ-5. The fuel consumption figures could certainly be improved with somewhat easier motoring and more careful driving in terms of speeds.

Getting back to the 18-point subjective evaluation list that we constructed, we were amazed that the scores by the three staff members who did the rating were so close. There were differences within the ratings but the total scores were very similar. Out of a possible perfect score of 90, the Toyota rated 60 and the Jeep rated 47. Because most of the subjective categories dealt with comfort rather than performance, it's natural that the Land Cruiser would be the high scorer. It is, all in all, far more comfortable than the Jeep. On the other hand, we should point out that the Jeep has the stronger performance and drives better.

Jeep CJ-5 and Toyota Land Cruiser at rest in their natural habitant. Only thing missing is a curious jackrabbit.

So, that's our comparison. As we stated in the beginning, we cannot tell you that one is better than the other. Both have their good and bad points, their strengths and weaknesses. In summing it up, we would rate the Land Cruiser the superior vehicle in terms of comfort and capacity and the Jeep CJ-5 the better performer. The Land Cruiser suffers mightly from the latest emission controls and does a lot of backfiring and exhibits considerable roughness in the engine. The Jeep, on the other hand, runs very well and has ample power and quickness. It does suffer from cramped quarters and difficulty in getting in and out for the larger driver. We like them both. They are what it's all about when it comes to getting out and doing serious "jeeping" as far as we're concerned. ●

The most famous 4-wheel drive vehicle of them all is now tougher and longer-lasting...believe it or not!

Some people believe a Jeep vehicle will last forever. So probably they'll expect this year's model to serve even longer. Because we've made it more rugged than ever. With stronger drive train components. Improved clutch linkage. Tougher tires. And a fuel tank skid plate. All as standard equipment.

This year, The Jeep comes with more style, too. The instrument panel is handsome to look at, easy to read. This is a vehicle built for adventure. More than thirty years of 4-wheel drive experience have made it dependable. Mighty Six and V-8 engines have made it powerful. And its high ground clearance and short overhang have made it maneuverable.

From any point of view, The Jeep is the winner and still the off-road champion of the world.

Toughest 4-letter word on wheels.

Jeep

Buckle up for safety... drive your Jeep vehicle with care and keep America the Beautiful.

OFF ROAD TEST

JEEP CJ-5

The American Jeep has been around for a good many years and until very recently there hasn't been a lot of exposure to the recreational buyer.

This newest contender on the off-road scene in Australia has one of the oldest and most respected names, and because of this you would expect to be purchasing a vehicle that, not only has benefited from all the years of being around, but also has that certain "something" that the other off-road vehicles do not!

When we look at the price of the latest range in Jeeps, we again think to ourselves this vehicle must be, and indeed after all these years should be, one of the best off-roaders in its price range.

The CJ5 basic, and we do mean basic, is $4195-60, and if you want a roof over your head it's going to cost you another $534-25 for either the hard or soft top.

The power pack in the CJ5 is a 232 CID six-cylinder engine capable of producing a gross torque of 215 lb.ft at 1800 rpm. The two-speed Dana type-20 transfer case takes the power from the all syncromesh, three speed gearbox and delivers it through a fully-floating hypoid-type open-end axle at the front and semi-floating hypoid-type axle at the rear. Both axles have 4.27 to 1 ratios.

Standard wheels and tyres are, in our opinion using too small a cross-section for off-road use. The Custom X-grip, tube type, 600 x 16 tyres are too narrow for the weight of the vehicle. On numerous occasions we encountered problems driving through road-side sand or soft dry dirt.

The kerb weight of the vehicle is almost the same as the original Jeeps supplied to the US army in 1941, and at 2450lbs the current registration for metropolitan NSW area is $179.00.

Stopping this weight is well taken care of by 11in x 2in drums all round and not once on the test did we encounter any problems at all with the braking efficiency, even in a quick stop.

The parking brake is a foot-operated pedal on the right of the accelerator. It requires a ton of weight to apply and when stopping on a hill it's a case of a quick jump of the foot from the foot brake to the parking brake, which can result in the vehicle rolling back. Hill starts, however, are no problem at all, and releasing the parking brake requires only the release (finger-tip touch) of a small lever under the dash on the right of the steering column. However, this lever *could not* be reached if lap-and-sash belts were fitted instead of existing commercial vehicles lap only belts. The outward appearance of the CJ5 is not unlike the old Willys Jeeps, and the body styling is both neat and pleasing.

Headlights are very good and there are four parking lights, two under the headlights and one more on each wing incorporating the turning flashers.

When the very heavy bonnet is lifted, it reveals an engine bay with plenty of room for maintenance (or the addition of a V8). The big six lays back slightly and on the drivers side are the oil filter, fuel pump and distributor, all within easy reach.

The other side of the motor is taken up by the air-cleaner, and the fuel vapor-control system.

The battery is set well up on the side of the engine bay and provided the bonnet is leaning on the windscreen, it is easy to fill and inspect. Standard electrical equipment includes, 37 amp alternator, two speed wiper/washers and hazard lights.

Getting into the vehicle is made easier by large steel steps, (which wipe off on rocks very easily), but once seated the steering wheel is uncomfortably close to the driver and the seat cannot be adjusted. Being this close to the steering makes manouvring in tight or bumpy off-road conditions very uncomfortable, if not dangerous.

The dash is enormous and the instruments are scattered across as if to take up as much room as possible.

Every instrument you need is there, including oil pressure, amps, speedo which incorporates the fuel and water gauges temp and warning lights for turning, high beam, oil and amps.

The facia is vertical and the instruments are not easy to read, but every thing is within easy reach of the driver and well lit at night.

Again, as in the CJ-6 seat belts and seating are totally inadequate. The belts are the lap-only type which result in the occupants not being restrained in a collision or in rough terrain. The seats give no support at all and the driver soon becomes tired without the support which is so important to his alertness on a long trip.

The brake and clutch pedals are still too high off the floor and the accelerator pedal is too far up the fire wall, creating an uncomfortable driving position which results in the foot creeping down the pedal. Constant replacing of the right foot is necessary on a long trip.

Passengers must make do with a single bench/bucket seat and half of the driver's double bench/bucket seat, and there are only seat belts for the driver and one passenger.

If there is seating for three, there should be seat belts for three!

The dash comes down very low and in the CJ-5 passengers are sitting with

RIGHT: With the back open and the tail-gate off, there is plenty of room for loading etc. The rear door, in the open position, results in bumps and abrasions about the head.

BELOW: The steering box is well exposed under the front bumper. This component is very fragile and could do with a little more protection.

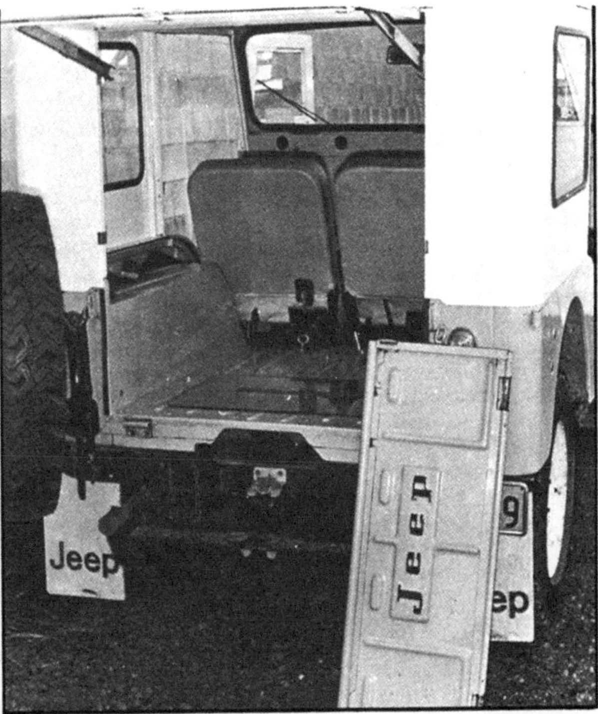

ABOVE: The drivers side of the engine is easy to work on but the other side is too cluttered. Battery is well up out of the way and makes for ease of maintenance.

ABOVE RIGHT: The jack etc are stored away under the drivers seat. If the rear of the vehicle is loaded it would be very difficult to get at.

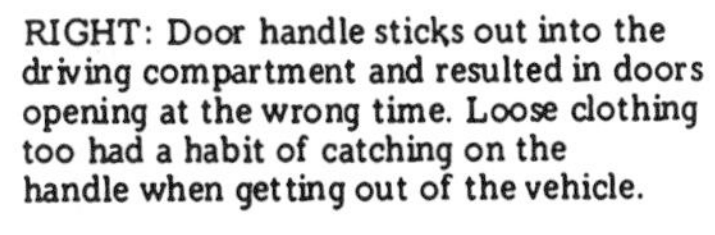

RIGHT: Door handle sticks out into the driving compartment and resulted in doors opening at the wrong time. Loose clothing too had a habit of catching on the handle when getting out of the vehicle.

FAR RIGHT: Towing equipment looks strong and comes as standard fittings.

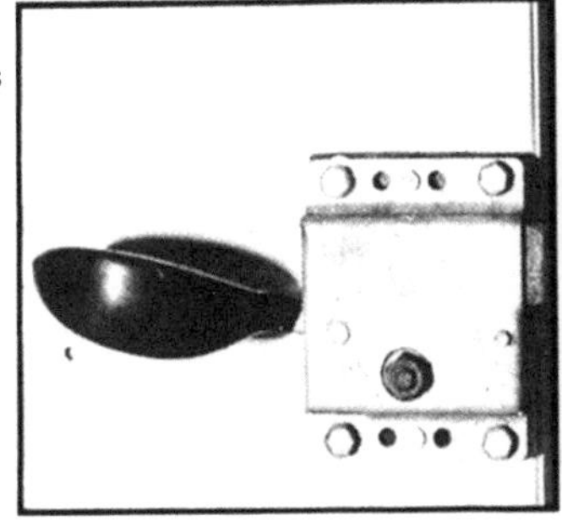

their knees about six inches away from it. Again in a collision or rough terrain this could result in a nasty injury.

The drivers door is locked with a key and once locked cannot be opened even from the inside. The passenger's door, however, can be opened from the inside even when locked. Consisting of a metal catch that slips under the handle, the passenger side lock is easily forced.

The door handles stick out into the cab a good inch and a half and on a trip of any distance passengers and driver tend to lean on the handle resulting in the door flying open. This happened on numerous occasions during the test period.

The windows are locked by particularly ineffective friction-catches which render the Jeep or its contents easy prey to the car-thief!

There is a single outside rear vision mirror which has to be adjusted every time the driver enters or leaves the vehicle. The canvas straps designed to stop the doors from swinging too far around are too weak, and on the second day of the test the passenger door strap broke and the driver's door strap became very slack. The result was that every time the door was opened it wiped out the mirror.

The rear compartment is roomy enough for tools, camping equipment etc but is not designed for extra passengers.

The windows in the side are very big and give good vision to the side for lane-changing and overtaking. The rear window is also very large. To open the tail-gate the spare wheel carrier must be swung to one side. Two telescopic arms support the door and hold it in the open position just level with your forehead. Loading and unloading the vehicle from the rear results in bumps on the forehead and on the top of the head. Even after the ten days of the test we were still hitting our heads on the door which should open another three or four inches higher.

The tail-gate can be dropped down and is supported by a strong chain on either side. It can also be taken off all together by simply pulling it out of its hinges. The tail-gate itself is very strong and could take quite a weight.

The rear lights are large and bright and incorporate a turning light, stop, tail and a reversing light. The lights on the left of the vehicle tend to be hidden on occasions by the spare wheel. However, Jeep Aust. has received ADR clearance allowing the spare to be relocated on the original mounting points on the right-hand rear body panel.

With its excellent power-to-weight ratio, the Jeep CJ5, for the farmer or builder etc, is a strong, reliable work horse.

But for the recreational buyer and the weekend off-roader there is so much more to choose from in other off-road vehicles. For reliability and strength the Jeep has a lot going for it, but for comfort and safety for the wife and kids, the recreational buyer can fill his needs with something a little less spartan.

The fuel comsumption for the short city hops varied between 11.8mpg (18.9km/g) 13mpg (20.9km/g) and on the open country highways we were averaging 13.9mpg (22.4km/g) with the best recorded figure of 15.5mpg (24.9km/g).

For most of the test period the CJ5 was loaded with camping equipment and carried four adults, and the on-road performance was quick and responsive as long as the vehicle was travelling in a straight line. Cornering however, was slow and the steering became heavy.

Because of the lack of support from the seats, the passengers and driver became tired after a short while and the lack of ventilation didn't help to keep the driver alert or active.

Off-the road the CJ5 is sure-footed and handling was comparatively easy. When driving on soft sand or loose dry dirt, however, it's another story. Because of the very standard narrow wheels and tyres, (6.00x16) on a couple of occasions we got hopelessly bogged and on one particular sandy spot the vehicle decided to take a rest and sat right down on the axles. Apart from this problem we found the CJ5 to be a strong responsive off-roader and even when we encountered trouble, the vehicle came through with a little coaxing and forethought and most of our off-road driving was without mishap.

due to the time lag between layout and publication there may be some variation with current prices.

PARTS

Front axle (left and right)	$125.91
Rear axle (left and right)	$ 76.48
Gear Set	$ 97.15
Exhaust (complete, 3-pieces incl. muffler)	$ 64.32
Front indicator/park lamp	$ 11.68
Front indicator/lens only	$ 6.33
Front guard (left)	$103.02
Front guard (right)	$130.95
Rear guard (left and right)	$133.72

OPTIONS:

Soft top with doors (CJ5)	$391.00
Soft top with doors (CJ6)	$441.00
Meyer Hardtop (CJ5)	$620.00
Meyer Hardtop (CJ6)	$657.00
Roll Bar (fitted)	$ 74.00
Bull bar (fitted)	$ 52.00
Winch (PTO)	$620.00
Freewheeling hubs	$102.00
Registration and third party	$151.16

Warranty 12 months or 12,000 miles.
Current prices: $4495 (CJ5); $4895 (CJ6).

RENEGADE ROADTEST

Continued from page **48**

an extra $4.05. This is another option you must take. It should be worth it to most owners with a vehicle equipped with cast aluminum wheels. That spare could get ripped off pretty fast without it.

The stock factory roll bar is a good unit and is well braced. It is unobtrusive with the top up and creates no problems for passengers getting into the rear seat.

If a few custom touches are your bag, the Renegade should surely make your little heart go pit-pat. With the "Renegade" hood stripe, the black-out hood and the wild paint jobs, it is a mean looking machine. The American Racing wheels help too. We saw quite a few heads turn as we drove ours around the streets of Los Angeles, and especially off-road. Our test vehicle had the orange paint, but, on a recent visit to a local Jeep dealer, we noticed a Renegade sitting in the showroom all shiny and polished. It was plum colored. That might sound like a weird color, which was our own reaction when we first heard of it. But looking at that rig sitting on the carpet, we got itchy fingers to get behind the door. A Renegade can do that to you. □

• For years, the very word Jeep has been synonymous with rugged dependability and go-anywhere-ability. The new CJ-5 Jeep makes that tradition even stronger. When American Motors took over as builders of the Jeep, they set several goals for an all-new model; the CJ-5 is the manifestation of those objectives. Among the changes are such items as availability of the AMC 304 V8, power steering, power brakes (all of which our test car had) and the ability to turn in a smaller circle.

Our test car also included such options as a skid plate, a Whitco top (which was excellent), deluxe passenger seat, full instrumentation and even the convenience of an ashtray.

The test session with the vehicle began with a drive around town. The CJ makes an excellent runabout, thanks to its ultra-quick maneuverability and relatively short 84-inch wheelbase. (A 104-inch version is also available.) Power steering made the parking a snap; however, we felt that fewer turns lock-to-lock would be helpful with the power assist. We next turned out onto the highway to head for one of our off-road playgrounds. On the freeways, the Jeep is out of its element. Above 55-60 mph, the vehicle becomes somewhat twitchy and the exceptionally low final gearing makes things sound a little busy. The CJ is still capable of cruising at high speeds for hours; in fact, we've seen Jeeps pulling trailers, but it's not their strong point.

As soon as we turned off the road, the Jeep came into its own. In a word, it's great. It could go almost anywhere and was stopped only by lack of proper tires for deep sand. It felt like it could climb a vertical wall. The new CJ-5 Jeep is still the standard by which all other off-road vehicles are judged—and the standard just became a whole lot tougher. ■■

JUMPING V8 JEEP

The new CJ-5 Jeep gets go-anywhere power with the addition of an American Motors 304-cubic-inch V8 option

Four-wheel drive was easily engaged with the transfer case and the Warn hubs. The result was sure-footed traction for cornering on sand, driving through deep mud or climbing rocky ground.

There is plenty of room under the hood for the American Motors 304-cubic-inch V8. An air pump and the associated plumbing make things a bit complicated-looking for novice mechanics.

JEEP CJ-5 LOVERS who swear by the lineal descendant of the World War II herotruck were aghast when engineers of the Jeep Division of American Motors Corporation elected to lengthen the CJ-5's wheelbase by a full 20 in. to create the CJ-6. What? A long wheelbase Jeep? Sacrilege! Heresy! "It ain't really a Jeep, y'know."

The CJ-5 vs. CJ-6 controversy started in 1955, the year Jeep introduced the CJ-5, and the CJ-6, too, for that matter. The CJ-5 then was on an 81-in. wheelbase, and the CJ-6 boasted 101 in. between wheel centers. In 1972, Jeep folk were astounded as the manufacturer lengthened the CJ-5's wheelbase to the present 84 in., and the CJ-6 was stretched to 104 in., in order to accommodate American Motors Corporation powerplants.

Historically, CJ-5s have an enviable sales record. The CJ-6 however, has *not* sold like hotcakes. Why? Is the CJ-6 not a Jeep, then? Is the CJ-5 enthusiast badmouth valid? Is the CJ-5 the only *true* Jeep?

These questions, plus a strong desire to look for answers are what brought about this head-to-head road test of the two vehicles, CJ-5 and CJ-6. Test driving was over the most challenging desert and mountain terrain that Southern California has to offer.

The Jeeps were driven hard through the dry sandy silt of the Colorado River delta, granite boulders and ironwood snags of flash flood drywashes, mesquite covered undulating dunes of windblown desert plain, washboard and chuckhole of mountain roads, loose shale, running streams, hub-deep mud as

CJ-5 vs. CJ-6

BY DAVE EPPERSON

Jeepers, it's really more than just 20 inches longer...

PHOTOSBY D. EPPERSON, D.HUNN AND L. MORLEY

slippery as toothpaste, high altitude snow and ice, stumps and logs—and the Friday evening recreational exodus traffic of California freeways. That's roughing it all the way.

CJ-5: THE STANDARD

The test Jeep CJ-5 supplied to PV4 was powered by the AMC 258-cu-in. Six with single-barrel carburetor, an optional powerplant, next one up in the line from the basic 232-cu-in. Six. The large displacement Six delivered power to the ground through the standard 3-speed manual transmission and 3.73:1 axle ratios. The test CJ-5 was not fitted with a locking rear differential. Suspension was comprised of the standard 7-leaf semi-elliptic springs at the front, 5-leaf semi-elliptics at the rear, and shock absorbers. Goodyear H78 x 15 Suburbanite XGs were mounted on standard OEM steel wheels. The CJ-5's front axles carried a pair of Warn free-wheeling hubs. The standard Jeep's short, stubby body featured a hinged tailgate, and the spare tire and wheel side-mounted to the right rear.

A cigarette lighter, a right-hand outside rear view mirror, a draw bar, a passenger grab handle, instrument panel padding and a dealer-installed Whitco vinyl top were non-standard items fitted to the basic Jeep. The sticker price of this unit out West was $5044.

Apple green paint, with black top, white wheels and the short wheelbase, gave the CJ-5 a perky, jaunty funtruck look, yet failed to totally disguise the tough-war, hard-work ancestry of all Jeeps past and present.

The 6-cylinder powerplant gave the CJ-5 respectable acceleration—sufficient for a reasonably quick 19.8-sec. quarter-mile at a 68-mph terminal speed. Only two gears of the 3-speed box were required to achieve the 0-60 time of 15 sec. flat. There are a good many V-8 powered passenger cars that won't match the off-the-line performance of this little Jeep.

The CJ-5's very conventional 11-in. diameter drum brakes, along with those cleated Suburbanites, on clean dragstrip asphalt surface, hauled the Jeep to a stop in a truly efficient 122 ft. There was some squaling protest; there was some smoke; and there was some loss of directional control toward the end of the panic stop test. However, it can be said unequivocally that the CJ-5 stops—NOW! ►

CJ-5 vs. CJ-6

CJ-6: MORE THAN 20 INCHES

The Jeep CJ-6 used for this comparative report was powered by the optional AMC 304-cu-in. V-8 with two-barrel carburetor. As with the short-wheelbase Jeep, the CJ-6's powertrain included the standard 3-speed manual gearbox and 3.73:1 axle ratios. And the CJ-6 was optionally equipped with a Trac-Lok differential at the rear. Moreover, the CJ-6 was factory fitted with a heavy-duty suspension system that included 10-leaf semi-elliptic springs and huskier-than-standard shock absorbers. Like the CJ-5, the CJ-6 was Suburbanite shod, and wheels were standard OEM steelies. The CJ-6 did not carry free-wheeling front hubs, and no tailgate was fitted.

The cigarette lighter, along with an AM radio, right-hand outside mirror, rear seat, spare tire/wheel lock, passenger panic handle, rear seat, instrument panel padding, spare tire mounting where the tailgate should have been, and black vinyl top from Whitco were the options that brought the CJ-6's West Coast sticker price to $5363.

Not quite fire engine red paint, black top and white wheels weren't sufficient to render the CJ-6 as seeming anything other than a Jeep distorted lengthwise. A gas pump jockey, looking at the CJ-6, asked, "Why did they make it so long?" The immediate thigh-slapping rejoinder was, "So it gets there a foot quicker."

If anything, the CJ-6's 20 in. of additional length contributed to a pickup truck appearance that is less recreation-oriented, much more farmyard utilitarian in nature than the general mien of the CJ-5. The CJ-6 simply doesn't have that distinctive short-coupled Jeep look—that so-cute-you-want-to-pet-it presentability that has attracted generations of Jeep lovers.

Looks, however, do not always equate with performance. The CJ-6, with its small displacement AMC V-8, managed the standing-start quarter-mile in 18.5 sec., at 74 mph. The 0-60 time was a very respectible 11.9 sec. For a 4wd vehicle with a dowdy truck look, this is more than acceptable acceleration.

And with brakes and Suburbanites, identical to those on the CJ-5, on the same pavement, the CJ-6 was panic stopped in a phenominal 135 ft. This stop was made with no fuss, no smoke, little noise and in a very straight track. The CJ-6 also is a NOW-stopper.

HOW THEY HANDLE

The CJ-5 may be the standard among off-road vehicles, and it does look the part, but the CJ-6, with its non-traditional proportion and the effects of its revised length, may set a new standard.

The chief differences between the CJ-5 and CJ-6, mechanically, have been recounted above, but the variances aren't entirely mechanical. In handling, the CJ-5 has a shorter turning radius than the CJ-6, yet by feel alone, the CJ-6 driver expects

Tailgate, zip-open curtain make for easy loading of the CJ-5, left. CJ-6 setup makes cargo a problem.

PRICES

Basic list, FOB Toledo, Ohio
CJ-5 . . . . $4099
CJ-6 . . . . $4195

Standard Equipment: 232-cu-in. inline Six, 3-spd manual transmission, front bucket seats, electronic ignition, fuel tank skid plate, heater/defroster, 2-spd electric wiper/washers, 2-spd transfer case, backup lights, F78 x 15B tires, voltmeter and oil pressure gauge

GENERAL

Curb weight, lb (test model) 2745 (CJ-5), 3030 (CJ-6)
GVWR (test model) 3750 (CJ-5), 4000 (CJ-6)
Optional GVWRs . . . . none

Wheelbase, in. 84.0/104.0
Track, front/rear 51.5/50.0
Overall length 138.9/158.9
Overall height 69.5/68.3
Overall width 60.0
Overhang, front/rear: 24.5/37.5 (CJ-5), 24.5/25.5 (CJ-6)
Approach angle, degrees 30 (CJ-5), 29 (CJ-6)
Departure angle . . . 18 (CJ-5), 27 (CJ-6)

Ground clearances (test model):
Front axle 9.3 (CJ-5), 8.9 (CJ-6)
Rear axle 8.5 (CJ-5), 8.2 (CJ-6)
Oil pan 12.8 (CJ-5), 13.7 (CJ-6)
Transfer case . 13.8 (CJ–5), 13.4 (CJ-6)
Fuel tank 14.0 (CJ-5), 13.3 (CJ-6)
Exhaust system (lowest point) 10.0 (CJ-5), 9.5 (CJ-6)

Fuel tank capacity (U.S. gal) 15.5
Auxiliary tank . . . . none

ACCOMMODATION

Standard seats . . . . . . front bucket seats
Optional seats: full-width split front bench seat, $29; rear bench seat, $89

Headroom in. . . 35.5 (CJ-5), 34.8 (CJ-6)
Accelerator pedal to seatback, max: 43.5 (CJ-5), 45.1 (CJ-6)
Steering wheel to seatback, max: 19.1 (CJ-5), 21.5 (CJ-6)
Seat to ground: 38.9 (CJ-5), 38.1 (CJ-6)
Floor to ground: 21.2 (CJ-5), 20.5 (CJ-6)

Unobstructed load space (length x width x height) in.: 40.8 x 35.0 x 45.8 (CJ-5), 54.2 x 35.7 x 44.8 (CJ-6)
With seats in place . . . . 31.5 x 35.7 x 44.8 (CJ-6)
Tailgate (width x height) . . . . 35.0 x 13.8 (CJ-5)

INSTRUMENTATION

Instruments: speedometer, odometer, voltmeter, oil pressure, water temp, fuel gauge
Warning lights . . . . hazard warning
Optional . . . . tachometer, $49

ENGINES

Standard .... 232-cu-in. inline Six
Bore x stroke, in. .... 3.75 x 3.50
Compression ratio 8.0:1
Net horsepower @ rpm ..... 100 @ 3600
Net torque @ rpm, lb-ft .... 185 @ 1800
Type fuel required .. leaded or unleaded

Optional 258-cu-in. inline Six $69
Bore x stroke, in. .... 3.75 x 3.90
Compression ratio 8.0:1
Net horsepower @ rpm ..... 110 @ 3500
Net torque @ rpm, lb-ft .... 195 @ 2000
Type fuel required .. leaded or unleaded

Optional 304-cu-in. V 8 .... $126
Bore x stroke, in. .... 3.75 x 3.44
Compression ratio 8.4:1
Net horsepower @ rpm ..... 150 @ 4200
Net torque @ rpm, lb-ft .... 245 @ 2500
Type fuel required .... unleaded

DRIVE TRAIN

Standard transmission: .... 3-spd manual
Clutch dia., in. 10.5
Transmission ratios: ....
3rd 1.00:1 (Six), 1.00:1 (V-8)
2nd .... 1.74:1 (Six), 1.83:1 (V-8)
1st .... 3.10:1 (Six), 2.99:1 (V-8)

Synchromesh .... all forward gears

Optional 4-spd manual $129*
Transmission ratios: 4th 1.00:1
3rd 1.41:1
2nd 2.41:1
1st 4.01:1
Synchromesh ..... 2nd, 3rd & 4th gears
*Available only on CJ-5 with 258-cu-in. 6-cyl engine. Not available on CJ-6.

Rear axle type .... semi-floating hypoid
Final drive ratios: 3.73:1 & 4.27:1
Overdrive .... none

Free-running front hubs $85
Limited slip differential $69
Transfer case .... Dana 20 2-spd
Transfer case ratios ... 2.03:1 & 1.00:1

CHASSIS & BODY

Body/frame: ladder-type frame and separate steel body
Brakes (std): 11 x 2-in. drums, front and rear
Brake swept area, sq in. 276
Swept area/ton (max load) 122
Power brakes (V-8 only) $45

Steering type (std) .... recirculating ball
Steering ratio 24:1
Power steering $149
Power steering ratio 17:1
Turning circle, ft 32.9 (CJ-5), 37.8 (CJ-6)

Wheel size (std) .... 15 x 5.5
Optional wheel sizes: 15 x 7 aluminum alloy
Tire size (std) .... F78 x 15B
Optional tire sizes: H78 x 15B, HR78 x 15B, H78 x 15D

SUSPENSION

Front suspension: semi-elliptic leaf springs on live axle with tube shocks
Front axle capacity, lb 2200
Optional .... none
Rear suspension: semi-elliptic leaf springs on live axle with tube shocks
Rear axle capacity, lb 3040
Optional .... none
Additional suspension options: HD shocks and HD springs, front and rear, $40

This is really all an owner needs for hard core Jeeping.

his vehicle to turn more tightly than the CJ-5. That it doesn't, however, is reflected in the fact that its wheelbase is longer than those of the Ford Bronco and IH Scout. Stability is the key to that certain feeling of turning-at-speed security. The CJ-6 can be slid, yanked, cranked and leaned well past the point at which the prudent driver would, in simple perspiring fear, let up on the CJ-5's accelerator pedal to avoid an abrupt roll-over.

The CJ-6's stability was apparent at an indicated 90 mph on a dusty washboard desert road. This speed seemed wildly insane to the driver of the CJ-5, which was unable to keep up, yet the long wheelbase Jeep CJ-6 seemed rock steady to its driver. That extra 20 in. seemed to suck up the chuckholes, smooth the washboard, and permit the torque of the V-8 to be transmitted to the ground in terms of sheer speed.

The CJ-5 remains a mountain-man's runabout for tight going, for ledge crawling, and snaking between fallen trees and slithering around mudholes.

The CJ-6 is an all-around off-roader's Jeep, capable of handling the open country at speed, giving away a trifle in tight trail maneuverability in order to achieve the aforementioned wheels-down, solid stability.

In sand, the test CJ-6 offered the most effective traction, probably for the reason that it was fitted with a locking rear differential. In two-wheel drive, the CJ-5 was forever getting stuck in sand, or the least bit of wet earth, which necessitated a jump out of the cab to lock the front hubs, and a change to four-wheel drive, and perhaps even low range four-wheel drive, in order to become unstuck. The CJ-6 could remain in two-wheel drive and motor out of the sticky stuff with tractive effort divided evenly between its two rear wheels.

On undulating terrain–the whoop-de-doos–the heavy-duty suspension of the CJ-6 offered control that appeared a significant improvement over the jump-and-chop of the lightly sprung CJ-5. The stiffer spring rates of the CJ-6 prevented bottoming-out that plagued the CJ-5 in some of the rougher going. Indeed, the CJ-6's 10-leaf springs withstood some mountain hardrock pounding that caused the right rear spring on the CJ-5 to take on a pronounced sag.

In slow, rocky climbs, the CJ-5, with the less twitchy horsepower availability of its 6-cylinder powerplant, proved the easier to control of the two vehicles. However, in mud, the lack of a locking rear differential caused the CJ-5 to hunt from side to side more quickly than the CJ-6. And, in the soup, the on-demand horsepower of the CJ-6's V-8 was a welcome benefit.

In boulders, sand and stumps, and ironwood and mesquite trash that litters a typical granite drywash, the short wheelbase CJ-5 tended to its crawling duties with great effectiveness where the CJ-6 driver took care not to bottom-out on projecting rocks, more of a danger with the longer wheelbased vehicle. Lack of attention could waste a very costly catalytic converter–which is standard with the no-lead-fueled V-8s this year. The extended wheelbase of the CJ-6 makes a great many more components vulnerable to sudden demise through increased opportunity for high-centering.

In fuel mileage tests, the CJ-5's Six looked better than the CJ-6's V-8 at round-town and 55-mph freeway driving consumption at 16.0 and 14.4 mpg, respectively. However, PV4 staffers are like any other city folk who must drive their funtrucks to off-pavement play areas–it takes hours in the toughest kinds of automotive congestion, and sometimes, through impatience, a driver's foot becomes heavy to the point of moderate illegality. Thus, it was discovered that at speeds in the 65-70 mph range, the CJ-6's V-8 is fractionally more fuel efficient than the CJ-5's 6-cylinder engine. At higher-than-legal►

speeds, the CJ-5's Six is forced to operate with carburetor secondary jets open, where the V-8 is still loafing along on its primary jets. The Six's fuel economy suffers accordingly.

The steering of both CJ-5 and CJ-6 was slow; the comment all-around among PV4 staffers was that power steering with fewer wheel turns lock-to-lock would be of great benefit to CJ-5 and CJ-6 drivers. As far as steering effort went, the CJ-5's steering proved lighter in feel than that of the CJ-6, which probably was a function of the extra weight of the CJ-6's larger, heavier engine.

The CJ-6 demonstrated a pronounced understeer in sand and gravel running, and the driver was forced to muscle the wheel hard to maintain his line. With 4wd engaged, the understeer is correctable with application of power, along with increased steering pressure. In 2wd, power alone does the job.

By comparison, the CJ-5 showed relatively neutral steering, but had a tendency to yaw after initial application of steering force. Any radius of a curve tended to be a series of small S-bends, right-left, but more right than left to negotiate a right-hand bend, for example. Therefore, hanging fuel cans, another spare, or heavy tools off the rear of the CJ-5 would probably compound this see-saw problem and take the Jeep's steering into the realm of the definitely hairy.

V-8 horsepower and heavy-duty suspension in the CJ-6 made things tough when the CJ-5 was assigned to run No. 2 in a two-Jeep convoy. The CJ-6 in the lead could rip along over the rough terrain, with it's suspension smoothing out the worst of it, while the CJ-5 had to be thrashed unmercifully in an attempt, not always successful, to keep up. The CJ-6 could be run in one gear, making use of the broad torque range of the V-8, while the CJ-5 driver was forced to prod the Jeep along with the gearshift lever, up and down the 3-speed range, to make use of the Six's narrower power band.

The Six offers plenty of torque, but not enough to run head-and-head with the V-8. The V-8 in the CJ-5 would be a dynamite combination—if the steering slows and wanders could be cured with power assistance and appropriate steering damping. After all, CJ-5s, with Chevy V-8s and quickened power steering, long have dominated some of the 4wd classes in off-road competition. It may be possible, through selection of a CJ-6, with proper engine and suspension options, to purchase off that friendly local AMC dealer's showroom floor what almost amounts to a desert racing stormer.

During PV4's road test run, the CJ-5 and CJ-6 were taken to altitudes in excess of 9000 ft. Both the Six and V-8 powerplants performed well in the thinner atmosphere. Neither showed a tendency to load up or to blow black smoke, which are conditions often encountered with sea-level-tuned vehicles in mountain running. Staffers attributed this high altitude performance to the leaner mixtures that are part of the engine emissions control systems installed on today's vehicles.

THE SMALL STUFF

The two Jeeps under road test both were fitted with standard side steps. PV4 staffers agreed the chief redeeming feature of these items is that they can be easily unbolted, removed completely and pitched in the nearest trash receptacle. These steps proved hinderances to entry and exit of the vehicles, collected mud and slush in the gooey going, and were nasty little shin barkers as well.

Without silver super tape, the Whitco tops and side curtains would have been unbearable in freeway travel. The Jeeps' rear ►

TWO JEEPS: A RACER'S VIEW

Longer means faster in off-road going...

BY DAVE EPPERSON

IF YOU WANT to know about Jeeps off-road, ask Gene Hightower." That was the advice given and taken by PV4's staff, in seeking an expert opinion on 1975 Jeep CJ-5 and CJ-6 off-road capability. Hightower is a long-time Jeep off-road racer. His opinions on Jeeps carry plenty of weight.

Hightower lives in Blythe, Calif., an agricultural center on the Colorado River, just a bridge's length from Arizona, in the middle of the great desert lands of the southwestern United States. The terrain surrounding Blythe comprises loose, silty sand dunes, hardrock drywashes littered with the debris of flash floods, undulating desert, low hills, precipitous serrated mountains, narrow canyons and boulder-strewn alluvial fans. All of this makes the true off-roader pant a little in anticipation of challenging vehicular sport. This stark, dry, hot, hard land is where Gene Hightower learned to drive.

In the Army, in the late 1940s, Hightower learned about Jeeps. "When I get back home," he told himself, "I'm going to put a V-8 in one of these things." Ex-soldier Hightower did just that. In 1955, he acquired a 1946 CJ-2A and bolted in a Chevy forked-8 powerplant. "In those days," Hightower grinned, "we used to chase wild horses across the desert. That's the way I learned to read the ground."

Those early "reading" lessons paid off later on. For Hightower, Jeep competition in the '50s and early '60s was merely the occasional sand drag. However, when the first Baja 1000 off-road race was contested, in 1967, it was Gene Hightower who finished first in class. In the 1968 running of the 1000, Hightower was

leading the Jeep class competition by five hours–until a broken frame put him out of the race at Villa Constitution. Hightower has competed in the Mint 400, the Stardust, the Parker 400, the Baja 500, the you-name-it in off-road competition, and even in the famed Pikes Peak Hillclimb, in which with a desert vehicle, he placed third in class in the uphill road race.

In short, Hightower has raced in 'em all. He has run enough Jeeps at a proper rate of speed over sufficient rough terrain for an appropriate number of years–in winning style–to eminently qualify him as an expert in Jeeps, starting where the pavement ends.

HIGHTOWER OFF-ROAD TESTS

Knowledge of his expertise prompted PV4 staffers out for a desert road test thrash with a couple of Jeeps to pay a call on Hightower. The desert racer was asked to drive both the 1975 CJ-5 and 1975 CJ-6, the former with the 232-cu-in. Six, the latter with the 304-cu-in. V-8, both with 3-speed manual transmission and 3.73:1 rear axle ratios, and factory installed OEM steel wheels with Goodyear Suburbanite H78 x 15 XGs all around. Evaluation runs were made over sandy, brushy dunes and up the side of a giant dune, used by Blythe locals for sand drag competition. Hightower was in his element. Were the Jeeps?

Hightower was asked to try the CJ-5 first, as it is a machine close to being the "standard" for this class of vehicles.

The racer fired up the Six, dropped the CJ-5 in gear and blasted away in the loose sand–squirting silt from all four. He took a run around some clumps of mesquite, cut some donuts in deep sand and got the Jeep airborne over a sand hummock of moderate size. Then he hit the sand drag hill, in low range, 4wd, at about 30 mph. The CJ-5 ran out of frijoles about half way up the super steep sand hill. Hightower backed down and offered his views on the CJ-5.

"Boy, there's no way that these tires are adequate for sand running," was his first comment.

Then he got into his performance evaluation. "The brakes are okay, and it handles well–but if it had power steering, it would be better. Double shock it, and it would be a race machine. Well, not really. This one would be nice for a farmer. It needs more horsepower for racing.

"Did you see that one time on the hill when it loaded up. Another spring on the carburetor would fix that," Hightower said.

Returning to power requirements for off-road work, the race driver said, "Horsepower is absolutely necessary in off-road racing. I had a 396 Chevy in a CJ-5, and led the Baja 500 with it until a rear axle broke." Obviously, Hightower's view was that the CJ-5 with the Six was down on horsepower and, for him, proved inadequate for modest desert running, let alone competition.

Then it was the CJ-6's turn for the Hightower treatment. First the racer dropped to his hands and knees for a look underneath the vehicle.

PV4 staff members had been worried about possible departure of the CJ-6's new (and expensive) catalytic converter in sudden, inadvertant contact with a rock. However, Hightower fretted about another low-hanging item. "I can't run this one too hard, or I'll break that oil pump.

Hightower then climbed into the CJ-6, ignited the engine and powered away, this time dusting bystanders with roostertails of silt from the four driven wheels.

He carried out his run through the hummocks and the donut runs, but avoided the jump for fear he would crunch one or the other of the valuable essentials underneath the vehicle.

Then he took his 30-mph, low range, 4wd, swoop at the sand drag dune–and rammed the CJ-6 to 80 percent of the sandhill's height, almost doubling the uphill distance achieved by the CJ-5.

PV4 staffers figured that Hightower had done his thing and that he would come in and report his findings. Not so. The racer continued to make dune whoopies, flying up the giant sandhill in a great arc, letting centrifugal force hold him to the hill, preventing gravity from pulling the Jeep downhill in a series of rolls. The driving performance was breathtaking.

Finally, Hightower came down off the dune, grinning widely, obviously delighted with the CJ-6's performance. He backed up his grin with, "Hey, this thing is all right."

Bear in mind that Hightower's view is from a race driver who has regularly piloted CJ-5s powered by big-inch Chevy or AMC powerplants.

"This one is really capable of doin' it," Hightower chortled. "This is the one I'm going to build next." Enthusiasm is a pale word for Hightower's reaction to the CJ-6.

"I didn't think the extra wheelbase would make that much difference, but boy it gives you better traction, and better handling all around–and it rides smoother."

And, he added, "I wouldn't have believed it, but the longer wheelbase helps in the turns. You can make turns tighter in the CJ-6 than you can in the CJ-5 without tipping over."

LIKES THE CJ-6

Hightower's final comment was that the CJ-6, with the AMC V-8 engine, would prove a more effective competition weapon than the CJ-5 in races such as the Parker 400. This is because the longer wheelbase would permit higher speeds over desert roads and off-road terrain that make up the California/Arizona rough race course.

Then PV4 staffers went their way, with Hightower's invitation to visit again, and perhaps take an extended off-road trip with the Hightower family. "And let me drive the CJ-6," was his parting shot, in itself the ultimate evaluation of the two vehicles. •

TEST MODEL

CJ-5, 258-cu-in. Six, 3-spd manual transmission, Calif. emission cert., cigar lighter and ash tray, outside passenger mirror, draw bar, passenger safety rail, padded instrument panel, Whitco top, free-wheeling hubs, 3.73:1 axle ratio

CJ-6, 304-cu-in. V-8, 3-spd manual transmission, HD springs and shocks, AM radio, cigar lighter and ash tray, outside passenger mirror, spare tire lock, rear bench seat, padded instrument panel, rear spare wheel mount, Calif. emission cert., 3.73:1 locking rear axle

West Coast list price (includes $357 freight): $5044 (CJ-5), $5363 (CJ-6)

Figures listed are for CJ-5 and CJ-6 respectively.

ACCELERATION

Time to speed, sec:
0-30 mph 3.9, 3.6
0-45 mph 7.9, 7.0
0-60 mph 15.0, 11.9
0-70 mph 21.9, 16.5
Standing start, ¼-mile, sec 19.8, 18.5
Speed at end, mph 68, 74

SPEED IN GEARS

High range, 3rd (3500 rpm) 82, 81
2nd (4000 rpm)............ 57, 54
1st (4000 rpm) 30, 31

Low range, 3rd (4000 rpm) 47, 46
2nd (4000 rpm) 28, 26
1st (4000 rpm) 14, 15
Engine rpm @ 55 mph 2150, 2200

BRAKE TESTS

Pedal pressure required for ½-g deceleration rate from 60 mph, lb 70, 75
Stopping distance from 60 mph, ft 122, 135
Fade: Percent increase in pedal pressure for 6 stops from 60 mph 18, 26
Overall brake rating ....excellent

INTERIOR NOISE

Idle in neutral, dbA 57, 66
Maximum during acceleration 87, 90
At steady 60 mph cruising speed ...84, 82

OFF PAVEMENT

Hillclimbing ability .... excellent
Maneuverability .... excellent
Turnaround capability .... excellent, ...very good
Handling...................very good
Ride.......................fair, good

ON PAVEMENT

Handling ....very good
Ride......................good, fair
Driver visibility......excellent, very good
Driver comfort ....good
Engine response ....very good

FUEL CONSUMPTION

Normal driving, mph 16.0, 14.4
Off pavement...............12.0, 10.8
Range, normal driving, miles 248, 223
Range, off pavement 186, 167

CJ-5 vs. CJ-6

side windows continually slat-slat-slatted loudly against top bow angle braces. Two strips of super tape across each brace and clear plastic window area reduced the billowing and beating to a mild rumble. And the front window zipper pulls jangled continuously against the exposed steel rods of the door crossmembers. Small squares of super tape fixed that.

The CJ-5 was equipped with deluxe doors, featuring automatic latching when the doors were pulled closed. Nice! The CJ-6, however, was fitted with doors that required manual operation of the latch lever to secure the doors in closed position. To close the left-hand door, for example, necessitated reaching the right hand across and over the left shoulder to swing the latch lever up, pulling the door closed and pushing the latch lever down—awkward to say the least. Jeep buyers would do well to select tops that have automatic latching mechanisms.

The CJ-6 was equipped with a rear seat that would accommodate two persons of moderate size. This was located all the way rearward in the vehicle's body, hence cargo area was between front seat backs and the rear seat.

As the CJ-6 was without a tailgate, it was necessary to load all cargo through the right front door, over the folded-forward right front seat, using an extended arm lift that would bring gladness to the hearts of truss manufacturers everywhere.

The CJ-5, on the other hand, was fitted with a zip-open rear window/curtain section that could be rolled up and secured in snap loops, plus a tailgate. Together, these features made a CJ-5 cargo loading, even the heavies, an easy breeze.

The '75 CJ-5 and CJ-6 both were fitted with fuel filler necks for unleaded gasoline, even though the CJ-5's 6-cylinder engine does not require the unleaded fuel. Because the filler neck is smaller in diameter and accommodates only the smaller diameter nozzle, now standard on pumps that deliver unleaded fuel, 1975 Jeeps with 6-cylinder engines cannot accept pump nozzles for "low-lead" or "regular" grades of gasoline, even though the latter are acceptable in the Six. This is a very important consideration for the off roader who may not be able to purchase unleaded fuel everywhere he goes. The owner of a 1975 Jeep with a Six could well consider modification, perhaps installation of a 1974 filler neck, or a reserve tank with its own filler.

In general, assembly of the Jeeps was neat, but not gaudy, about what a buyer would expect from a long-time Ohio truck works—nothing slick or trick, but everything well bolted together. Indeed, the CJ-5 shed only one bolt, from the dash panel, and popped only one tailpipe clamp in the rough going. Nothing shook loose on the CJ-6.

MONEY'S WORTH

Another way to compare the test CJ-5 and CJ-6 is to have another look at the sticker prices, and consider what the customer gets for his money. For $5044, the buyer receives a basic CJ-5, with the larger of two available 6-cylinder engines—and not much else, other than free-wheeling front hubs. For $5363, the buyer drives away in a CJ-6 with a V-8 engine that represents 46 cu in. of additional piston displacement, plus 50 additional lb-ft of peak torque, and 40 strong horsepower, along with husky heavy-duty springs and shocks, and a locking rear differential—and a radio. That's a whole lot of long Jeep for only $319 over the price of the almost standard CJ-5. In terms of what it would cost the average Jeep buyer who might finance his purchase through a bank on a 36-month contract, the added cost is about $10.50 per month in the ol' payment schedule. In terms of entertainment value, and in rough running capability, for the pure off roader, the ten bucks a month is definitely worth it.

CONCLUSION

The two-Jeep test run through desert and mountain told PV4 staffers why the CJ-6 hasn't sold well. It's simply because not enough serious off roaders have been exposed to the highly desirable all-terrain capabilities of this vehicle. It is staff opinion this situation is the result of pure prejudice on the part of dyed-in-the-wool "original" Jeep lovers who just can't stand change—even if it's for the better.

The CJ-6 is all Jeep, in every sense of the word and, in many instances, as PV4's road test crew determined, superior to the CJ-5 "original." The CJ-5 enthusiast badmouth of the CJ-6 is totally unwarranted hogwash. And, know this, the self-styled off-road ace who speaks ill of the CJ-6 doesn't know what he's talking about because he obviously never has driven the extended chassis Jeep in off-road situations.

Here's the long and short of it: The CJ-5 is not the *only* Jeep. The CJ-6 is a true Jeep—plus. •

To No-Man's Land in a CJ-5

Offered a CJ-5 Renegade with 401 cubic inches of V-8 by Randall Engineering, the staff gets its kicks . . . but Route 66 it wasn't.

by Spence Murray

Our self-imposed editorial board established hard-and-fast rules during planning stages of this book when we nixed travel stories due to space lack and the importance of delivering only "hardware" information. But be that as it may, we can't help but mix in this condensed cross-country tale. After all, it just isn't right for a desk-type to write about getting stuck, lost, upside down—or all three—unless he's done it once or twice. So, gather 'round and let us expound on an indirect route by 4X4 between the Phoenix area and Los Angeles.

THE RANDALL EXPERIENCE

As small as outskirt Mesa, Ariz., may be, it contains one of the West's more active dealerships. Randall American by name, they handle stock AMC and Jeep products in quantity. But a separate division, titled Randall Engineering (for reasons to be explained in a minute), can and will deliver any AMC Jeep engine/body combination; a pure hot rod shop.

Muscle *car* types delight in Randall's 401-powered Gremlins, a non-factory, Randall-only option. Too, muscle *4X4* types like their Jeeps big-motored, especially 401 V-8 motivated CJ-5's. Legislation (read smog laws) being what it is, it's quite illegal for a new-car agency to mate an engine and a chassis not certified to go together. But Randall *Engineering* isn't an agency.

Say you want one of the aforementioned 401-CJ-5's. Trot over to Randall American and buy a CJ-5, but opt for the Renegade package, which includes the 304 V-8, to save yourself money in the end. Sign the papers and take delivery. Now, you're the owner of the new rig, making it a used car through legal eyes. Next, drive over to Randall Engineering (100 ft. across the service area). There, they'll drop in the 401 V-8 (about 4 hours work), and relieve you of an even G-note in the process, giving you what we'll call a Stage I CJ-5. They could go up to a Stage II level if you want them to, by adding either a Borg-Warner close-ratio T-10 4-speed or AMC's version of the TorqueFlite automatic, neither of which is available in CJ's from Toledo. Or go all the way to Stage III and have them toss in full-time four-wheel drive and QuadraTrac. Also at hand are off-road tires and wheels of all types and sizes, blueprinted or fully modified engines, trick paint jobs—or anything else you might want to add.

Skip Randall, one of the Randall clan running the American/Engineering show, offered us a Stage I CJ-5. We felt it would be useful for many projects in this book: as an accompanying vehicle for a road test rig, a guinea pig for evaluating off-road accessories, or around town/desert transportation for your book staff.

PERFORMANCE PLUS

For the performance oriented, we later dyno-checked the CJ-5 at Cruse & Co., in Van Nuys, Calif., and found some surprises. The Lizard delivers 110 rear-wheel horsepower at 2500 rpm, 135 at 3000 rpm, and an unnerving 145 at 3500—up in Corvette territory! That All-Terrain rubber isn't the thing to be using on pavement acceleration runs, though, and we suffered much wheelspin (in two-wheel drive), but nonetheless stop-watched ourselves at 7 secs. flat for 0-60 mph. That's with the baseline CJ-5 3-speed manual trans, too, and 3.73:1 rear-end gears—the combo demanding slow shifts. The option of a 4-speed or Torque Command would surely have helped, but perhaps not without wide-base pavement tires to get a little bit better grip on the asphalt.

The basic CJ-5 package is a sturdy desert traveler. Add the Renegade options, Firestone All-Terrain-shod Jackman wheels, and a 401 V-8, and the rig becomes a real performer under any on- or off-road condition.

Induction on our conversion is by way of a 3310 single-pumper, dual-feed Holley—perhaps over-carbureted but nevertheless delivering 18 street mpg on the 73-mile *Motor Trend* magazine test loop of freeway, hills, high- and low-density traffic. All this in a 2500-lb. rig with 105 more horses (255 net) and 100 more lbs.-ft. torque (345) than the original-equipment 304 engine.

The ride home is the real point, and there wouldn't be much to tell if we'd simply traveled the I-10 between Phoenix and L.A. Instead we chose to head southward to the Gulf of California at the Mexican port of Puerto Peñasco (pop. 28,000) and road's end. Northwest up the coast and around huge Adair Bay there's another shoreside community at El Golfo de Santa Clara, handily shortened to El Golfo, housing some 500 hardy year-rounders eking a living from fishing and out of Arizona weekenders who meander down the 2-lane paved road from Yuma. Between Puerto Peñasco and El Golfo wanders an almost aimless shoreline, stretching 115 miles and inhabited, during cooler months, by a whole two people . . . at a camp not shown on maps but called Pancho's; where, for a fee, Pancho himself helps trailerites launch their boats after they've struggled 40-odd miles over a poor dirt road.

Other than Pancho's plywood high rises, the coastline is little more than 4X4 traps of gumbo mud, unseen (until you're into one) runoff arroyos where the Gulf retreats from inland marshes when the normal 28-ft. tide subsides, two bad (and one not-so-bad) headlands where the more daring can tippy-toe around boulders awash at low tide, and miles of hard-packed sand-and-shell beach closely backed up by sheer cliffs whose feet flood at high tide and which would very gladly trap the mired or broken-down vehicle.

SOME PRECAUTIONS

Normally, such an attempt should not be related where novices might take a similar idea into their heads and try to emulate the trip, endangering not only themselves but those who go out to find them in the event they don't return. In past years of wandering into these environs, by all manner of transportation (boats, planes, 2X4's and 4X4's, etc.), I've never met—or heard of—anyone driving overland between El Golfo and Peñasco short of riding the Mexican train that twice daily makes the run between the ports on its way from track's beginning at Mexicali to its juncture with the main north/south railroad at Benjamin Hill.

But let us explain that many people in L.A. and Phoenix knew our route and schedule, that my companion and myself had run a goodly part of the beach previously, and that if Skip Randall didn't hear from us in 48 hours (two-thirds the limit of our food and water) that a helicopter was ready with tools, gas, and medical supplies, and a pilot that knew the area.

On the other hand, though, 115 roadless miles weren't all that formidable, and I've driven the dirt between Tijuana and La Paz (before the paved road was built) five times, once setting an all-time low-elapsed-time mark—in a standard two-wheel-drive sedan. Experience, be advised, was at hand.

INTO THE WILDS

The tank was topped off at Peñasco, we dropped the 25-psi highway pressure of the Firestones to 12 lbs., shoved the stick into four-wheel High, and headed up a flat-out five miles of beach to an encampment at Punta Cholla.

The short-coupled CJ-5 felt as stable on the hard sand as it had on the macadam, four-wheel drive giving us good directional stability at speed.

Then, bluurrrccchhh! The Lizard mired itself. Sand fine as face powder but wet and with a consistency of 50-wt. oil buried us to the axle housings. Civilization was still visible on the horizon behind us. Ahead were 114 miles more of we knew not what.

"Un-sticking" oneself is discussed in another chapter, and it's easy to read and understand from an armchair. But when the Sonoran desert is glimmering under July's 130° F., and with humidity touching 90%, it takes a lot of mustering to belly down in oozing mire with trenching tool, scissors jack, and scraps of linoleum (found unaccountably nearby), and free some 2500 lbs. of CJ-5. Packing the linoleum and brush to form a base for the jack, we raised the All-Terrains free from the muddy vacuum, filled the voids with more brush, then backed until we mired again. Two more cycles of this and we were back on firmer terra and picked another way around the bog.

The perimeter of Adair Bay is best described as a curvilinear no-man's-land of glistening wet clay and hummocked sand. There's no line, really, separating one terrain from the other . . . the types overlap. Other than distant peaks poking their heads above the barren horizon, there is no visual relief. No motion to the air, just a blowtorch sun and a stark, lifeless expanse. Maps of the area are vague because of the tidal inundation. We had NASA photographs, though, courtesy Gemini 9. Taken at 400 miles altitude, few details could be made out save the extent of the bay proper and its "shoreline," which resembles a giant's toothy bite into a caramel sundae. But they served to keep us oriented. By keeping the ooze to the left, watching ahead for another bog, and picking our way around the sand hummocks that build around the roots of near-lifeless vegetation, we came at length to the Baja California *y* Sonora railroad that arrows between El Golfo and Puerto Peñasco. We'd wanted to avoid the tracks, feeling the steel link meant "civilization," but here we had no choice, for a few miles at least, and worked the Lizard onto the roadbed to bump over the ties. Soft mud "dry lakes" lay to each side of the rails; the right-of-way was the shortest—and only—way, about halfway around Adair Bay, to traverse the region.

RAILROADING IT

It's doubtful if anyone has written of CJ-5ing over railroad ties. It's irrelevant to off-road driving, it's illegal, it'll unwind the screws in your glasses, and you might be clobbered by a train. But if nothing else is at hand and it's vitally necessary to forward progress on a bona fide mission—as opposed to playing games—bear witness: A CJ-5's 84 ins. of wheelbase coincides with the spacing of railroad ties. When the front wheels drop off one, so do the rears. It's like driving up the Capitol steps, only level. Sometimes on a washboard road where a slow pace will wrack a chassis unmercifully, a faster one smooths things out. Not so on ties.

1

It's 3 mph, and four-wheel Low to reduce strain on U-joints and axles. Ker-blump, ker-blump, ker-blump, at about the speed you can say it out loud.

Way stations at about 20-mile intervals, consisting of a few hovels, a windmill and perhaps a couple of scrapped freight cars to house worker's families, are the only inhabited communities in this desert's awesome interior.

We ker-blumped into one at dusk, startling a herd of goats and unnerving their herder. The good man made us understand that from the nameless station a dirt road of sorts did, indeed, lead southward to the Gulf. We had cleared the bite of Adair Bay and could head Gulfward again.

TAKING ANOTHER TRACK

The "road" evolved through infrequent cross-desert travel by the way station's fish eaters, traveling in decrepit cars that would be refused by an L.A. junkyard. But these hardy souls, reading the terrain as you and I do a book, often carve their own way when an earlier-formed trail becomes suspect from dune encroachment or upwelling water. Thus, tracks branch in all directions, sometimes rejoining the "main" trail a little later, sometimes disappearing as into thin air. We followed along for some distance but when the sky grew a moonless black, the track we'd been following simply vanished. Rather than continue, we bedded down there and then; it would be senseless to circle and try to pick up the trail and waste precious gas.

If everything else failed, the Gulf lay a few miles ahead and, going against the hard-and-fast rule to stay with an immobilized vehicle, we could hike to the coast and signal one of the Mexican fishing boats that ply northern Gulf waters near shore.

But, at length, we topped a dune and were at water's edge, back at last on a stretch of hard-packed beach literally covered with dinner plate-sized shells. El Golfo lay 20-odd miles to the right, northwestward up a beach which we had driven before.

At the encampment of Pancho's, the summertime place-watcher gave us 30-wt. coffee, considered the Lizard (and us too, I suppose: two *locos* there in the July heat), and confirmed that El Golfo now lay only 28 kilometers (about 18 miles) further away.

The CJ-5 had crept through the desert in four-wheel Low, but now on harder, flat sand we up-shifted into four-wheel High and roostertailed up the strand at a steady 50 mph. The beach alternated between semi-soft and semi-hard, and at times, to maintain that progress, the 401 was floorboarded and laboring; at others it took the same easy throttle pressure that pavement would.

"WHY?"

Within minutes the low shade trees that mark El Golfo out of that yellow vastness wriggled above the shimmering horizon, and soon we were driving on pavement once again. We topped a near-dry tank with Pemex, re-inflated the tires to 25 psi and sat down for a cool beer. We hadn't proved much—except that the Lizard was easily up to the task required—but the ordeal seemed worth it when a Mexican asked where we'd come from and we responded, "Puerto Peñasco." Raising his eyebrows in surprise he queried, *"Por que?"* "Why?" Neither of us could think of an answer.

1. Swapping an AMC 401 V-8 for the 304 that is part of the Renegade package isn't that easy, though the engines are outwardly similar. Front sheetmetal was stripped to aid conversion, made by Randall Engineering in Mesa, Ariz.

2. Start of our desert crossing was at Puerto Peñasco, Sonora, Mex., where severe Gulf of California tides allow beaching of fishing trawlers for annual repairs. Ships are idle during summer, when extremely warm water sees fish leave area for several months.

3. Once around the gumbo of Adair Bay, travel was along beach, but jutting points of land mean occasional trip inland to pass the low capes.

4. Much of the northern Gulf coast is backed by bluffs, reached by the waters of high tide. Get immobilized here and your vehicle is as good as gone. High tide at this point is several feet above the top of the CJ-5.

2

3

4

JEEP CJ-5

Four-wheel driving's "old man" makes up in off-roading what it lacks on.

BACKGROUND / Say "four-wheel drive" to most people and the automatic response will be "Jeep." And when you say "Jeep," it's the CJ-5 model that comes to mind. No wonder, since it's probably the single most recognizable vehicle in the world today, with the possible exception of the VW Beetle. That's understandable, because current CJ Jeeps still have a definite resemblance to the first military models built. In the nearly 35 years since then, various Jeep models have penetrated to every corner of the earth. This explains why their squarish, functional profiles are familiar even in countries where 99% of the people couldn't tell a Chevy from a Ford!

The CJ initials stand, logically, for "Civilian Jeep"; all M-series models have been built for military use. The basic CJ-5 and slightly longer CJ-6 were introduced 20 years ago. They replaced CJ-3B models, which had flat hoods, square fenders and generally squared-off body lines, much like the M38 military unit. The CJ-5 and CJ-6, then as now, featured a more rounded design, but had an F-head 4-cylinder engine under the hood.

CJ-5 Jeeps today don't look much different than those of 20 years ago, but they have undergone important mechanical changes. The last, and most important, came in the 1972 model year. American Motors 6-cylinder and V-8 engines replaced the 4-banger (which became available only in export models) and V-6 formerly used under all CJ hoods. The new engines dictated some chassis and driveline changes.

GENERAL/Since the 6's and V-8's were longer, wheelbases were stretched 3 ins. to accommodate them. The CJ-5 wheelbases went from 81 to 84 ins.; the CJ-6, from 101 to 104 ins. The hoods and front fenders were also lengthened, increasing overall length by 6.5 ins. for both models. At the same time, front tread width was boosted a full 3 ins., from 48.5 to 51.5 ins. Rear tread was widened from 48.5 to 50 ins. The wheelbase and tread changes combined to produce greater stability both on and off pavement; they remain the same for '75.

The 1975 lineup includes standard CJ-5 and CJ-6 models, plus the Renegade—which is merely a CJ-5 with custom trim, accessories and a 304-cu.-in. V-8 as standard equipment. Maximum gross vehicle weight rating (GVWR) for the CJ-5 is 3750 lbs.; for the CJ-6, it's 4000 lbs. All CJ models for 1975 require no-lead gasoline, but only the 304 V-8 has a catalytic converter. Jeep managed to squeeze its 6-cylinder engines in under smog control regulations without using converters. Engineers came up with a modified intake manifold that allows operation with a leaner air/fuel mixture, which helps reduce emissions and also improves fuel economy and throttle response.

CHASSIS/CJ Jeeps have extremely rigid frames designed to cope with the demands of rugged off-pavement driving. Side rails are of fully boxed construction and the ladder-type frame has no less than six strong crossmembers. Frames of '75 models have side rails of increased gauge thickness for added strength.

Suspension is by semi-elliptic leaf springs in both the front and rear. Deflection rate of the standard front springs is 190 lbs. for the CJ-5 and 210 lbs. for the CJ-6. Rate of the standard rear springs for both is 230 lbs. Heavy-duty springs, with deflection rates of 270 lbs., are available on the front and rear of both vehicles.

Drum brakes are used both front and rear in the CJ series. They measure 11 ins. in diameter by 2 ins. wide. Front disc brakes are not available, but power assist is optional with the drum system in CJ models with 304-cu.-in. V-8 engines. All brakes are self-adjusting.

Up front, there is a Saginaw recirculating ball steering gear. Steering ratio is 24:1 for the standard manual system, and it takes five turns of the wheel to go from lock-to-lock. When Jeep lengthened the CJ models for 1972, it also switched to a new Dana 30 open-end front axle. Gross axle weight rating (GAWR) of the full-floating axle is 2200 lbs. Turning circle diameter is 32.9 ft. for the CJ-5, 37.6 ft. for the CJ-6. GAWR for the rear axle of both is 2700 lbs.

DRIVELINE/The standard CJ engine—except for Renegades—is a 232-cu.-in. 6-cylinder unit with a single-barrel carburetor. It's teamed with a 3-speed fully synchronized transmission. Optional engines include a 258-cu.-in. 6, which comes with either the standard 3-speed or an optional 4-speed manual gearbox. It also has a single-barrel carburetor and the same bore—3.75 ins.—as the 232 6, but a longer stroke: 3.9 vs. 3.5 ins. Compression ratio is 8:1 for both.

The largest engine offered is a 304-cu.-in. V-8; it's standard in Renegades and optional for other CJ models. It has a 2-bbl. carburetor and 8.4:1 compression. It comes only with the 3-speed manual. Sorry, but there's no 4-speed or automatic transmission for the V-8. Jeep design engineers say that the extra case and tailshaft housing lengths of these two boxes, when installed behind the 304 V-8, would necessitate a too-short driveshaft with consequent severe U-joint angles. However, we've seen several custom installations which have suffered no U-joint problems.

A Dana 20 transfer case with a low-range ratio of 2.03:1 is used in the drivetrain. Final drive ratios are 3.73:1 standard and 4.27:1 optional.

The most notable engine improvement, aside from the modified intake manifold mentioned earlier, is an all-new electronic ignition system. It eliminates points and condenser, provides a stronger spark and drastically reduces maintenance requirements.

Jeep has not yet extended its full-time four-wheel-drive system to the CJ line. Again, it would be a matter of too-severe U-joint angles.

BODY/Bodies have remained the same since they were stretched slightly—all in the cowl area—to cover the increased wheelbase. CJ Jeeps are available only in the familiar open configuration, but full- and half-cab metal tops are optional. Whitco also designed a new convertible soft top for them for 1975. The full tops are more durable, the company claims; they also have improved visibility and larger door openings than earlier tops. They come in black and white or the new Levi's tan or blue when ordered with the "Levi's package."

Standard seats are chair-like buckets covered with black or buff leather-look vinyl. A matching rear bench seat is optional. Levi's interiors feature seats covered with vinyl cloth that looks just like the cloth used for the famous Levi's jeans. A rear bench seat and front buckets in the material are standard in Renegades, optional for other CJ's.

TEST VEHICLE/Our test vehicle was a 1975 CJ-5 with a 258-cu.-in. 6-cylinder engine. As the photos show, it had

2900

Jeep
2900

JEEP CJ-5

a standard interior and black convertible top. It had optional Warn locking front hubs, 3-speed manual gearbox, standard 3.73:1 axle ratios and optional Goodyear Suburbanite H78X15 tires.

The interior was spartan with only the necessities in evidence; but for the purpose little else was needed—although a radio would have been nice. The only luxury was a heater combined with a ventilation fan, although we used neither one. The vinyl bucket seats were comfortable and had enough padding for the skinniest of rears; however, adjustment was more than a one-handed operation. The seats are mounted to a bar which is attached to the body at one of several holes. If adjustment is desired, you must unbolt the seats and move them to a different mounting hole. Being long-legged, we could have used more rearward adjustment, but the seats were already back to their limit—41 ins. of legroom. If time had permitted, we could have modified them for more stretch, but with an overall vehicle length of only 138.9 ins., room for expansion is at a premium. The floor is spacious and uncluttered except for the stubby transfer case lever.

It has been wisely said—probably by a Jeep veteran who by now is sadder but wiser—that whatever you do in a CJ-5, do it in a straight line. The short, top-heavy rigs literally feel, to the novice Jeep driver, like they're on the verge of tipping over. Not necessarily true, for the standard CJ (as our test vehicle) will go to at least 41° before tipping. But it would be easy to turn the steering to full lock, then wind up the engine and slam the clutch out—*presto!*, right on your side. It should hastily be added, though, that the sanely driven CJ, once its short-wheelbase peculiarities are gotten used to, is about as safe as any vehicle.

Prospective CJ buyers—those who have not put much mileage on one—should be alerted that while some 4X4's are designed primarily for highway use but with off-pavement capabilities, that others are primarily off-pavement rigs with at least some highway capabilities. The CJ happens to be one of the latter.

The test rig was a pretty basic CJ-5. The wheels were standard steel types. It had the standard, side spare tire mount, not the optional swing-out rear carrier, and no rear bench seat, though these weren't missed. An option we would liked to have had was the reinforced roll bar. Either a factory roll bar or a good aftermarket unit is excellent insurance against injuries in case of accidents. Even a full roll cage should be considered for an open 4X4 to be used for really rough off-pavement work.

OBSERVATIONS/The CJ-5 tested weighed in at 2850 lbs. with full gas tank. Since its GVWR was 3750 lbs., that gave it a reasonable payload capacity of 900 lbs.—plenty for even a hefty driver and passenger, plus a useful amount of camping equipment, tools and other gear. Or for four people with the optional rear bench seat, which doesn't leave a lot of room for carrying things. Adding such options as the heavier V-8 engine, air conditioning, a winch and other accessories could cut substantially into that payload capacity. We've seen CJ-5 Jeeps dolled up with so many weight-adding goodies that they topped the maximum GVW rating with just two people aboard! That's something to consider for anyone planning to buy a CJ.

CJ Jeeps are strong little vehicles and may be more capable than most of handling occasional overloads—but it's not advisable to exceed maximum GVWR figures with any car or truck. You only can lose, in terms of accelerated wear for many components, impaired handling qualities and reduced braking capability.

We liked the new voltmeter—replacing the old ammeter—since it shows battery condition and whether the alternator is functioning properly; we also liked the fact that an oil pressure gauge, not an idiot light, is standard equipment—and has been since the mid-'74 model year.

ON-PAVEMENT/The speedometer dial is partially blocked by the steering wheel when you're driving straight ahead, so it's difficult to keep accurate tabs on your speed. This isn't important off-pavement, when you're usually going rather slowly anyhow, but it's a real drawback on the highway.

One member of the test crew complained that the vehicle was "noisy, drafty and rough (like a boat) on the highway, but for off-pavement use it's hard to beat." When told that today's CJ models are considerably more civilized than those of just 4 or 5 years ago—when wheelbases were shorter, steering more difficult, standard 4-cylinder engines made highway driving at then-current speed limits virtually impossible, and soft tops were draftier and offered poorer visibility—he just shook his head!

It's true that a '75 CJ still doesn't give anything approaching a passenger car ride or comfort on paved roads, but it's still a step up from earlier models. The ride is choppy, as might be expected given the short wheelbase and sturdy suspension. It obviously isn't the ideal choice for long distance touring. On the other hand, around town at typical urban/suburban speeds, its deficiencies in riding quality aren't as important or noticeable. And its convenient size makes it a nimble car in traffic, as well as easy to park. It would be plenty adequate as a second car for many families, since the 6-cylinder engine should deliver up to 20 mpg after a few thousand break-in miles have been registered.

OFF-PAVEMENT/A CJ-5 is really in its element, however, when it leaves paved roads. It churns over trails or desert sand washes like a baby tank—and is equally at home in mud and snow if shod with the proper tires. The Polyglas Suburbanites with which our test CJ-5 was fitted make a reasonably good compromise for on/off-pavement driving, especially if the accent is on pavement use much of the time. A real four-wheeling enthusiast who plans to "do it in the dirt" much of the time would be better off with a set of more specialized tires suited to the terrain he frequents.

Due to its rather high center of gravity and tall seating position, the

BOX SCORE

Each of the following factors was rated on a scale of 1 to 10, as: Poor, 1 to 2. Fair, 3 to 4. Good, 5 to 7. Excellent, 8 to 10. An 8-point award, for example, was given if the category warranted better than a GOOD rating, but not the highest of EXCELLENT. Each book staff member compiled his own Box Score, then averages were drawn accordingly. Here's how the Jeep CJ-5 stacked up.

Factor	Score
On-pavement handling/performance	5.0
Off-pavement handling/performance	8.3
Maneuverability	8.7
Stability	5.3
Acceleration	7.0
Gearing	8.5
Braking	8.0
Hillclimbing ability	9.0
Prolonged travel comfort	3.7
City travel comfort	5.7
Interior access (front seat)	6.3
Rear seat access (if applicable)	N/A
Load space access	6.7
Engine access	8.3
Engine splash shielding	8.0
Instrument/controls layout and access	7.3
Visibility	9.0 (w/o top)

CJ-5 seems to threaten a tipover frequently on sidehill going or in soft sand, particularly when ruts are wide and deep. The threat is often more imagined than real, but a Tilt-O-Meter to indicate when body lean is close to the danger point is a wise addition—along with a roll bar.

The 2.03:1 ratio of the transfer case in four-wheel-drive low range, coupled with the standard 3.73 axles, provide plenty of low-speed traction and pulling power for most situations. For those who plan to work a CJ-5 hard—such as for serious snow plowing using the optional plow blade available—or in hilly country where it's often necessary to creep up and down steep grades at low speeds, 4.27:1 axles might be preferable. They provide more engine-compression braking on downhill runs, which takes some of the load off the drum brakes.

TRAILER AND RV USE/Jeep says that any standard CJ-5/6 model is capable of towing trailers up to 2000 lbs. fully loaded with no special equipment. Properly equipped, it gives its blessing to towing trailers weighing up to 5000 lbs., with tongue weights up to 750 lbs. The 304 V-8 is recommended for trailers above 3500 lbs., and an extra-duty cooling package (which is standard in air-conditioned models) is suggested for anything above 2000 lbs., as are 4.27 axle ratios, the largest optional tires, heavy-duty suspension, and power steering and brakes.

From personal experience, we suggest that trailers of 20 ft. or less in length are the best matches for CJ Jeeps—and that longer-wheelbase CJ-6 models are more suitable for trailers of that size and near the maximum weight of 5000 lbs.

SUMMATION/Despite some shortcomings, the CJ Jeeps are beguiling vehicles. They're tough, durable and dependable—and current models are probably the best all-around units ever offered. The range of AMC powerplants available has been a big improvement; lack of adequate power (for most conceiveable uses) is no longer a problem. Options already mentioned, and others—from a steering column-mounted tachometer to CB radios—make it easy to tailor a CJ for any work/recreation use.

Changes made by American Motors over the past 3 years have upgraded CJ Jeeps slightly for pavement driving, without cutting back on the rugged qualities that earned them deserved fame for off-pavement use; they have a lot of charisma, to boot. That, and their ability to withstand the roughest kind of driving conditions, makes it easy to overlook some of their drawbacks in terms of creature comforts. They still remain the standard of the entire 4X4 world!

JEEP CJ-5—GENERAL

Curb weight (lbs.)	**2850**
Payload (lbs.)	**900**
Track (ins.) front/rear	**52/51**
Overall length (ins.)	**141.5**
Overall height (ins.)	**72**
Overall width (ins.)	**70.5**
Overhang (ins.) front/rear	**23.5/34.5**
Ground clearance (ins.):	
Mid-wheelbase	**10**
At lowest differential	**8.5**
At lowest chassis point/component	**8.5/diff**
Approach angle (degrees)	**38**
Departure angle (degrees)	**32**
Floor height (ins.) front door	**21.5**
Floor height (ins.) tailgate	**27**
Tailgate width (ins.)	**37**
Tailgate height (ins.)	**14.7**
Cargo length (ins.) w/rear seat (N/A pickups)	**N/A**
Cargo length (ins.) w/o rear seat	**37**
Cargo width (ins.) extreme	**55**
Cargo width (ins.) between wheelwells	**36**
Cargo height (ins.) (N/A pickups)	**46**
Steering (turns lock-to-lock)	**5**

ENGINES

	Displacement (cu. ins.)	Bore (ins.)	Stroke (ins.)	Compression ratio	Net hp @ rpm	Net torque @ rpm
Standard	232 6-cyl. (1-bbl.)	3.75	3.50	8.0:1	100 @ 3600	185 @ 1800
Optional	**258 6-cyl. (1-bbl.)**	**3.75**	**3.90**	**8.0:1**	**100 @ 3500**	**195 @ 2000**
Optional	304 V-8 (2-bbl.)	3.75	3.44	8.4:1	150 @ 4200	245 @ 2500

DRIVETRAIN COMBINATIONS

Engine	Transmission	Transfer case	Axle ratios
232 6-cyl.	3-speed manual	**Conventional**	**3.73**/4.27
258 6-cyl.	**3-speed manual** 4-speed manual		
304 V-8	3-speed manual		

CHASSIS

Model	Wheelbase (ins.)	GVW's (lbs.) Stand.	GVW's (lbs.) Opt.	Turning circle (ft.)
CJ-5	**83.5**	**3750**	N/A	**32.9**
CJ-6	104.0	4000	N/A	37.6

Brakes Stand.	Brakes Opt.	Tire sizes Stand.	Tire sizes Opt.	Steering Stand.	Steering Opt.	Fuel capacity (gals.) Stand.	Fuel capacity (gals.) Opt.
Drum	Power	**H78X15**	N/A	**Conventional**	Power	**15.5**	N/A
Drum	Power	H78X15	N/A	Conventional	Power	15.5	N/A

BASE PRICE
(FOB factory. Manufacturer's suggested retail.)

Model	Price
CJ-5	$4099
CJ-6	$4195

TEST VEHICLE PERFORMANCE

Fuel consumption (mpg)—on-pavement	**14.3**
Fuel consumption (mpg)—off-pavement	**4.0**
On-pavement acceleration: 0-30 mph (secs.)	**5**
On-pavement acceleration: 0-55 mph (secs.)	**13.5**
Rear wheel horsepower @ 2500 rpm	**68**
Rear wheel horsepower @ 3000 rpm	**70**
Rear wheel horsepower @ 3500 rpm	**60**

Emissions at idle: **170** HC parts per million; **2.0%** carbón monoxide.

● Certain equipment, option combinations may not be available in some areas. See your dealer.

JEEP CJ~5 from Volkswagen

CAR test

The immortal Jeep — virtually a Mk 3 version of the military general-purpose vehicle which became famous in World War 2 — has never really got going in South Africa in any volume. But now that it has joined the Volkswagen stable in the Republic, it could be heading towards the top.

The story of how the Jeep (now built in America by American Motors Corporation, successors to Kaiser-Fraser and Willys-Overland) came to be a VW model in South Africa is a story on its own: in short, VWSA has been awarded the franchise by AMC to build and market the Jeep range, starting with the CJ-5 (short wheelbase) and CJ-6 (long wheelbase) models.

So in this country it has been coming off its own assembly line at VWSA in Uitenhage since August, and is being sold and serviced by 50 selected outlets in the wide VW dealer network.

The modern Jeep is very different from its famous wartime predecessor: much bigger, heavier and more powerful. It started growing in 1955 when the bonnet line was raised to take the higher F-head 4-cylinder engine. Later the wheelbase was lengthened 88 mm by AMC after it took over Kaiser-Jeep in 1970, so as to house the AMC six-cylinder engine.

The old side-mounted spare wheel mounting gave way to a hinged bracket at rear, and both wheels and tyres became bigger.

So while today's Jeep still has elements of the original boxy military shape, it stands higher and has become more truck-like in its handling.

There is very little of the original Jeep left: at a quick check we would say that the rear load/seat body, the handbrake, the "donkey gear" transfer case and the T-clip spring-loaded bonnet catches are the only bits which have survived without much change. Everything else, from windscreen to wheels, and from brakes to steering mechanism, has evolved during production in the past 30 years.

FUNCTIONAL COMFORT

The original Jeep was designed to be built as quickly and cheaply as possible, and to work as efficiently and reliably as possible till it became cannon fodder.

The peacetime concept — which has been adopted by other manufacturers of 4-wheel-drive vehicles as well — is to produce a rugged and comfortable go-anywhere vehicle with broad usefulness and appeal. It should be adaptable for military use, agriculture, engineering and surveying, hunting and fishing.

So the Jeep as built today has well-designed foam-filled seats, a comparatively high standard of body seal, and much more power. The small load space — which has plain metal double benches at either side — will take four people seated, or can be used as utility space. The windscreen can fold forward onto the bonnet for hunting and beach riding, and a sturdy bolt-on roll-bar is a worthwhile option. The clip-on vinyl soft-top canopy is neater and more effective than the old canvas top.

The war-time Jeep with its little 4-cylinder side-valve engine, three-speed gearbox and transfer case engaging low-range "donkey gears" had a drawbar-pull rating of something like 50 tons, and would pull a double-decker bus with ease.

The engine has doubled in size since then — current production uses a 3,8-litre AMC six-cylinder unit in low-compression form, producing 88 kW at 3 600 r/min, and with a tremendous torque output. This engine is really far too big for normal purposes — it makes the vehicle nose-heavy, and has necessitated the introduction of very low-geared steering (5 turns lock to lock).

The suspension is by live axles front and rear, with 4,09 to 1 diffs, multi-bladed leaf springs front and rear, with telescopic shockabsorbers all round.

KEY FIGURES

1 km sprint	39,1 seconds
Terminal speed	120,5 km/h
Fuel tank capacity	59 litres
Litres/100 km at 80	15,4
Fuel range at 80	382 km
Litres/100 km at 90	17,2
Fuel range at 90	342 km
Engine revs per km	1 775
National list price	R4 350

EXTRA GEAR LEVER

There are three gearlevers on the floor: the main three-speed gearbox for normal road use; the drive selector which engages either two-wheel or four-wheel drive — or disengages the transmission for power take-off purposes; and the transfer case selector which brings in the "donkey" ratio superimposed on the standard gearbox.

It looks a bit terrifying to the uninitiated, but in fact all the driver does for normal purposes is set the transfer case selector to "high range", at the same time selecting "two-wheel drive", and then use the all-synchromesh gear-

The big, slow-revving six-cylinder engine provides more power than usually needed.

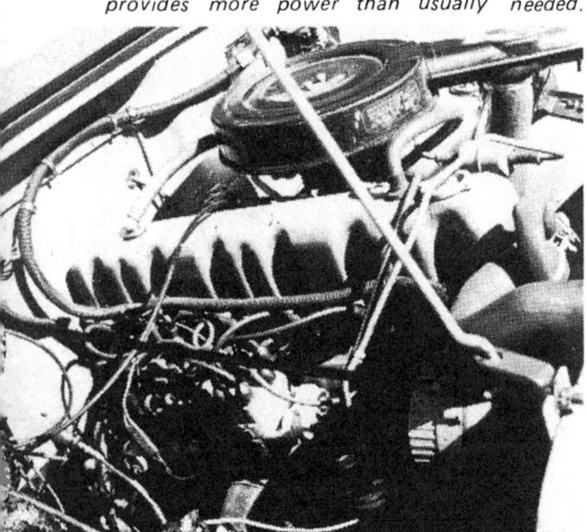

The T-clip bonnet catches are one of the few remaining features from the original Jeeps.

The spare wheel is mounted at rear on a bracket which swings clear for tailgate access.

With canopy unclipped and stowed away, the padded roll bar (a worthwhile option) is seen.

Controls and instruments are functional. In current production, a floor-mounted handbrake is used.

The soft-top vinyl canopy and doors provide reasonable weather protection and fair vision.

box in the ordinary way, forgetting about the other facilities: they are only for off-road and other specialised work.

DONKEY GEARS

The Jeep's gearing is interesting, if we tabulate it in km/h. Its normal gearing is car-like, while the 2,03 to 1 transfer case ratio introduces tractor-like undergearing through what becomes, in effect, an 8,3 to 1 final drive ratio:

	Low	High
km/h per 1000	**16,6**	**33,1**
1st gear	**19,8**	**40,2**
2nd gear	**32,1**	**65,3**
Top gear	**59,8**	**119,6**

The donkey-range gears are so low as to be almost redundant with this big engine — we did not find any situation on test which could not be handled by the normal (high range) 1st gear.

A refinement introduced in comparatively-recent years is free-wheeling front hubs: by operating turn-keys on the hubs themselves the hubs can be disengaged from the transfer case to eliminate front-drive "drag" in normal road use. In all our performance tests, of course, the front drive was left disengaged and free-wheeled.

PERFORMANCE

The Jeep feels very strong, though somewhat clumsy, in normal road performance tests. It develops mild wheel-spin in a hard start from rest, and turns in some pretty tidy figures: 0-100 km/h inside 20 seconds, 60-80 overtaking in 3,7 seconds, and a top speed potential of nearly 130 km/h.

With the big 7.00 x 15 heavy-lug tyres fitted on the test vehicle, though, it became a bit of a handful at speed, and showed comfortable (if rather noisy) cruising ability at about 80 km/h.

The engine tended to run hot when worked hard, and the floor at the back became decidedly warm under the influence of the exhaust system.

Gradient ability is tremendous, of course — even in top.

ECONOMY AND BRAKING

With six big cylinders working hard in a surprisingly-heavy vehicle (1,7 tons!) no-one should expect the Jeep to be economical: under optimum conditions (level tarred road, free-wheeling front hubs, light throttle) we recorded 15,4 litres/100 km (18,3 m-p-g) at 80 km/h, and this rises to 17,2 litres/100 km (16,4 m-p-g) at 90.

The 59-litre tank gives it fair range under these conditions, but if lower ratios and four-wheel drive are in use, of course, consumption would rise even further. Over a period of several days, covering 285 km, we recorded 20,1 litres/100 km (14,0 m-p-g) in general road use.

The Jeep has unboosted big drum brakes all round, and showed remarkably consistent stopping ability — though the pedal is hard and it takes some stopping from higher speeds.

HANDLING AND RIDE

The big wheels, heavy tyres, drum brakes, drive joints, and diffs on beam axles create a very high unsprung mass on this unusual vehicle, so that ride is rather juddery and heavy-feeling. There is a lot of mechanical and canopy noise (fluttering), and strong arms and legs are needed to manage controls properly.

The Jeep wanders at speed, and leans fairly heavily in turns. The steering column is spring-loaded to reduce shock, and a lot of winding is needed in hard turns, with a poor centring action: usually the car has to be steered back into the straight-ahead line.

Instruments are set to the left, near the centre of the fascia, and are not easy to read when driving.

It is a high-standing vehicle, bigger than it looks, and rather cumbersome to handle by normal road standards. Getting in and out of the driving seat needs some agility, owing to high stance, fixed sides and low-set steering wheel.

AT ITS BEST OFF-ROAD

But take it off the road, into sand, rocks and mud, and the Jeep is like a duck taking to water. Suddenly it becomes responsive, graceful and manageable, biting firmly, pulling strongly, and riding the most appalling terrain comfortably.

It has a spectacularly-short turning circle to get it out of tight situations, and the driver — sitting well back, almost over the rear wheels — has a clear view in all directions. This is what the Jeep was designed and built for: it is tremendously tough, powerful and capable, and will claw its way through, up or down almost anything.

A disc on each of the front wheel hubs is rotated by hand to introduce free-wheeling of the front drive — another useful option.

SUMMARY

There is nothing fancy about this big-hearted vehicle: it has no heater, no interior light, and few items for comfort and convenience — though it does have essentials like outside mirrors and windscreen washer jets.

VWSA has announced that it will extend the range of options and special equipment for the Jeep progressively, including comfort items, implements, winches and hard-top (glassfibre) canopies.

This is a special sort of car with great potential, either as a work-horse with limited load capacity (its rating is half-ton) or as a fun-machine for leisure use. It was the first of the popular 4-wheel drives, and after 30-odd years it is still one of the best. ■

SPECIFICATIONS

ENGINE:

Cylinders	six in line
Carburettor	Carter single choke
Bore	95,25 mm
Stroke	88,90 mm
Cubic capacity	3 803 cm^3
Compression ratio	8,0 to 1
Valve gear	o-h-v, pushrods
Main bearings	seven
Aircleaner	dry twin element
Fuel requirement	93-octane Coast 87-octane Reef
Cooling	water — 10,0 litres
Electrics	12-volt AC

ENGINE OUTPUT:

Max power SAE (kW)	88 (118 b-h-p)
Max power net (kW)	75
Peak r/min	3 600
Max torque (N.m) at r/min	251 at 1800

TRANSMISSION:

Forward speeds	three
Synchromesh	all
Gearshift	floor
Low gear	2,997 to 1
2nd gear	1,832 to 1
Top gear	Direct
Transfer case	2,03 to 1
Reverse gear	2,997 to 1
Final drives	4,09 to 1 (front and rear)
Drive wheels	2-w-d rear; 4-w-d all

WHEELS AND TYRES:

Road wheels	15-inch pressed steel discs
Rim width	6,0L
Tyres	7.00 x 15 off-road heavy duty
Tyre pressures (front)	120 to 200 kPa
Tyre pressures (rear)	120 to 250 kPa

BRAKES:

Front	279 mm drums
Rear	279 mm drums
Pressure regulation	nil
Boosting	nil
Handbrake position	on floor

STEERING:

Type	worm and roller
Lock to lock	5,0 turns
Turning circle	8,0 approx metres

MEASUREMENTS:

Length overall	3,515 m
Width overall	1,539 m
Height overall	1,717 m
Wheelbase	2,121 m
Front track	1,308 m
Rear track	1,270 m
Ground clearance	0,175 m
Licensing mass	1 704 kg

SUSPENSION:

Front	live axle
Type	7-blade leaf springs
Rear	live axle
Type	7-blade leaf springs

CAPACITIES:

Seating	2 plus 4 (total 6)
Fuel tank	59 litres
Utility space	930 dm^3 approx

WARRANTY:
12 months or 20 000 km

TEST CAR FROM:
Volkswagen South Africa, Uitenhage.

ACCELERATION

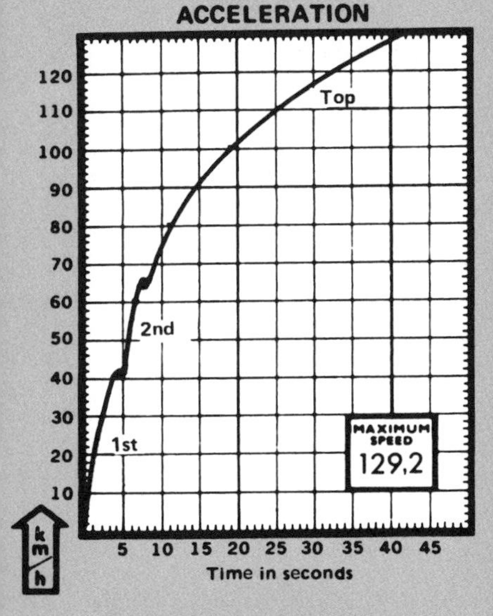

BRAKING DISTANCES

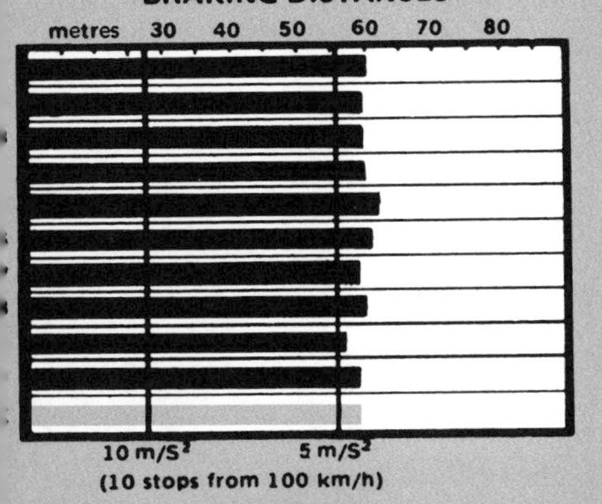

ENGINE SPEED

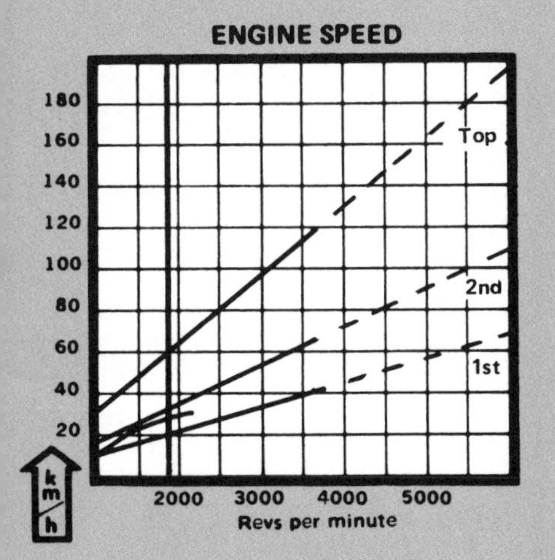

GRADIENT ABILITY

MAX. TORQUE 1800 RPM

1st
2nd
Top
30°
25°
20°
15°
10°
5°

(Degrees inclination)

test	JEEP CJ-5

PERFORMANCE

MAKE AND MODEL:

Make . . . . VW (AMC)
Model. . . . . Jeep CJ-5

PERFORMANCE FACTORS:

Power/mass (W/kg) net. 44,0
Frontal area (m^2) . . . .
km/h per 1 000 r/min (top) . . . 33,1

INTERIOR NOISE LEVELS:

	Mech	Wind	Road
Idling	50,5	–	–
60	79,5	–	–
80	84,0	–	–
100	89,0	89,0	89,0

Average dBA at 100 89,0

IMPERIAL DATA

ACCELERATION FROM REST (seconds):

0-50: 10,6
0-60: 17,0

MAXIMUM SPEED (m-p-h):

True speed 80,3

FUEL ECONOMY (m-p-g):

40 m-p-h 23,1
50 m-p-h 18,2
60 m-p-h 15,9

ACCELERATION FROM REST:

0-60. 6,6
0-80. 10,4
0-100. 19,0
1 km sprint 39,1

OVERTAKING ACCELERATION:

	2nd	Top
40-60	2,9	4,4
60-80	3,7	5,0
80-100		8,4

MAXIMUM SPEED:

True speed 129,2
Speedo reading 125

Calibration:

Indicated:	60	80	100
True speed:	64	84	104

FUEL CONSUMPTION (litres/100 km):

60. 11,3
80. 15,4
100 17,9

CRUISING AT 80

Mech noise level. . . . . 84,0 dBA
0-80 through gears . . . . . 10,4 seconds
km/litre at 80 6,5
litres/100 km 15,4
Braking from 80. . . . . 3,9 seconds
Maximum gradient (top) . . . . . 1 in 6,9
Speedometer error . . . . 5% over
Speedo at true 80 . . . . 84 km/h
Engine r/min. 2 420

BRAKING TEST:
From 100 km/h:

First stop. 4,8
Tenth stop 4,8
Average. 4,80

GRADIENTS IN GEARS:

Low gear . . . . 1 in 2,5
2nd gear . . . . 1 in 3,5
Top gear . . . . 1 in 5,4

GEARED SPEEDS: (normal)

Low gear 40,2
2nd gear 65,3
Top gear 119,6

GEARED SPEEDS: (donkey range):

Low gear 19,8
2nd gear 32,1
Top gear 59,8
(Calculated in km/h at engine peak r/min — 3 600.)

CAR October 1976

NOISE VALUES

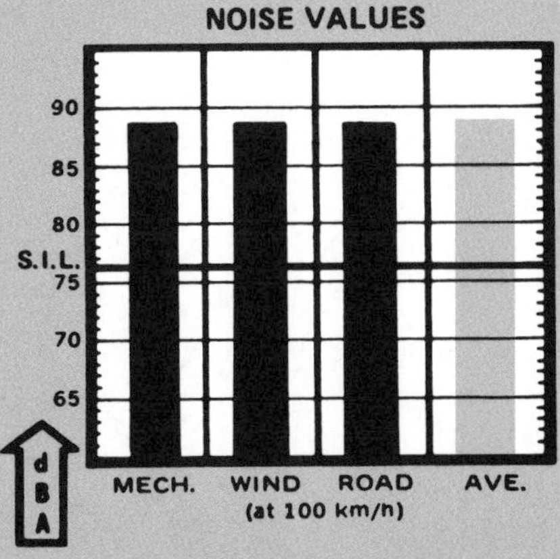

LUGGAGE CAPACITY
(dm³)

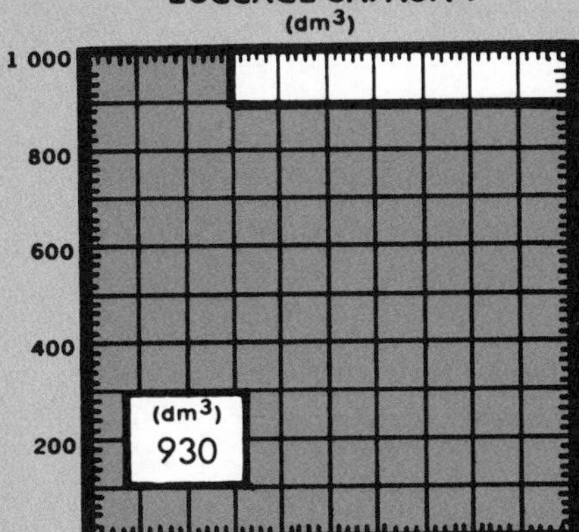

FUEL RANGE

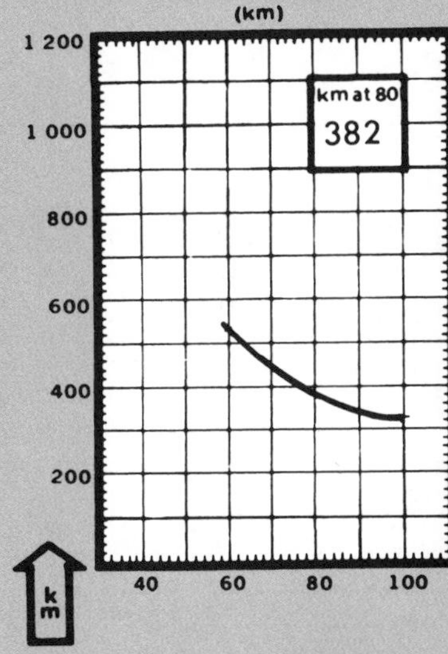

FUEL CONSUMPTION
(litres/100 km)

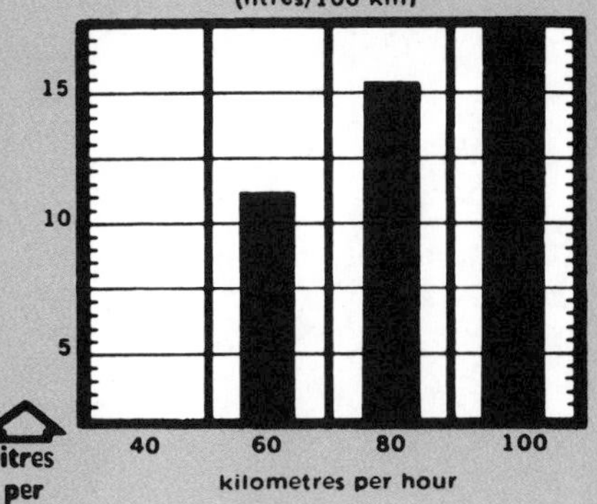

"I WOULDN'T SWAP..."

....a CJ5 owner who has spent a little time on his vehicle lent it to us for a while to look at, photograph and talk about. The result was this brief report that indicates that all that is Jeep, isn't necessarily bad!

LEFT: A big rear view mirror, Donaldson air-cleaner and a set of molded rubber guard flares. All worthwhile extras that add a touch of individuality to the vehicle.

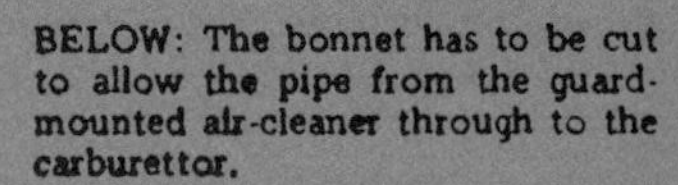

BELOW: The bonnet has to be cut to allow the pipe from the guard-mounted air-cleaner through to the carburettor.

The CJ5 Jeep has had its problems since introduction to Australia, not the least of which was acceptance by the public. It's a pretty spartan unit, relatively expensive and suffers from a bad PR rub-off as a result of the "bitsy" efforts at marketing before LNC Industries (or Jeep Australia) took over in 1974.

Many people have maligned the Jeep for many various reasons, and we were more than pleased when we met Tim Viner, a CJ5 owner, former truck driver and Landcruiser owner, who would not part with his CJ5 for any other four-wheel-drive.

He admits to having had his share of

problems - but nothing that couldn't be overcome with a little thought and a little effort. Everything he's had go wrong so far has been small - and easily fixed. Most of the problems he's fixed himself, and generally improved on those he couldn't do were looked after by Grenville Motors in Sydney.

The first changes to the Jeep were the replacement of the standard wheels and tyres with a set of Magnum alloy wheels and Pos-a-traction Stagger block tyres. That was almost 35,000km ago, and so far only one tyre needs to be replaced. That's not bad for what is basically an off road only trye.

The second non-standard item to be fitted was a very solid, and fully padded roll bar. This little investment, supplied by Off Road Equipment at Kogarah, certainly paid off. Several weeks after its installation Tim almost wrote off his Jeep when he back-flipped it off the top of a sand-dune at Kurnall on Sydney's southern beaches. If it hadn't been for the bar, he would not be driving the Jeep now. This incident meant a complete rebuild for the Jeep, and with it a complete respray. This was well worth it, as one of the early complaints was that the paint was very thin, and not all the panels matched.

The standard seats were the next to go, and these were replaced with a set of highback buckets from a Falcon, fitted to specially-built mounts. The rest of the modifications have been relatively straight forward...a few shims under the front end to improve the steering; a bull-bar and A-frame tow hitch, a swing-away spare wheel and jerry-can holder for the back and a set of nicely molded guard flares in heavy duty rubber. These are a far cry from those offered by Jeep Australia - they actually fit.

Two other problems which also come to light are brakes and exhaust system.

The linings fitted originally disappeared within a matter of a few thousand kilometres, and the original

ABOVE: The famous Frantz toilet roll filter! The filter uses a by-pass system.

LEFT: The standard seats aren't much chop. These high-backs are out of a Falcon.

BOTTOM: In case of emergency - grab it! There's also a level gauge to tell you just before you roll.

"I WOULDN'T SWAP..."

ABOVE: Additional lights and a big air-cleaner - worthwhile additions to any four-wheeler. RIGHT: The big Rambler motor and the Jeeps excellent power-to-weight ratio allows wheel-spin even in soft sand. BELOW: It's a multi-personality machine!

exhaust system rusted out but a few hundred kilometres later.

Since then the Jeep has been through one more exhaust and now has a modified system which exits just in front of the rear wheel arch. The greatest problems with the standard version were that the muffler continually rusted out, and that the long pipe (to the rear of the vehicle) kept breaking the exhaust mounting brackets. This appears to have been overcome by the shorter pipe.

Under the bonnet there have been very few modifications. The oil now runs through a Frantz by-pass filter and a Donaldson cyclopac air filter has been mounted on the left front guard and connected to the carburettor. Other than that the only other addition is a set of triple air horns.

Apart from minor things such as small areas of rust, initially poor paintwork, and the standard seats which don't support or adjust anywhere enough, this is one Jeep which has caused its owner very few problems - especially of the nature referred to by many Jeep owners we've encountered.